Setting up Home

Cassell Lifeguides

Cassell 'Lifeguides' are books for today's way of life. The increasing trend towards a 'self-help society' is an indication of the need for reliable, helpful information in book form, as less and less advice is offered elsewhere.

With this series, Cassell furthers its reputation as a publisher of useful, practical self-help books, and tackles subjects which are very much in line with today's lifestyles and problems. As people become increasingly aware that situations need to be looked at from all sides, they can turn to these books for realistic advice and encouragement.

Setting up Home by Fiona Buchanan
Living with Teenagers by Tom Crabtree
Coping with Separation and Divorce by Jean Stuart
Staying Healthy by Mike and Tricia Whiteside
Ready for School by Maggie Wilson

Setting up Home

Fiona Buchanan

CASSELL

Cassell Publishers Limited
Artillery House, Artillery Row
London SW1P 1RT

Copyright © Cassell Publishers Limited 1989

All rights reserved. No part of this publication
may be reproduced or transmitted, in any form or
by any means, electronic or mechanical including
photocopying, recording or any information storage
or retrieval system, without prior permission in
writing from the publishers.

First published 1989

British Library Cataloguing in Publication Data
Buchanan, Fiona
  Setting up home.
  1. Household management.   2. Residences, Removal
  I. Title
  640

ISBN 0-304-31665-2

Typeset by St. George Typesetting, Redruth, Cornwall
Printed and bound in Great Britain by Courier International Ltd., Colchester

Grateful thanks are due to Mr William Compton, plumber and handyman;
Mr K. Walker of Bourneville Landscapes; David Whitehouse Design Consultants;
Nottinghamshire Trading Standards; The Electricity Council and British Gas.

Contents

Introduction   1

1. Finding and buying your new home   3
   Finding the right area   5
   Paying a visit   7
   The home-buying process   11
   Setting the wheels in motion   12
   Mortgages   13
   The role of the solicitor   14

2. Moving day and security for the home   17
   MOVING   17
   Taking the strain out of packing   18
   Removal firms versus DIY   18
   The move   20
   Rewarding refreshments   21
   SECURITY   22
   Which lock to choose   23

3. Settling in and getting on with the neighbours   26
   Getting the job done   27
   Neighbours   28
   Open house or sanctuary   30
   Other visitors   31
   Building up a social life   32

4. Relationships: coming to terms with living alone or in a new partnership   34
   GOING SOLO   34
   Entertaining and eating well   36
   Sharing with a lodger   38
   Finding the right person   41
   Pets   43
   COUPLES   44
   Sharing the load   47

        Your social life   48
        When things go wrong   49

5. **Furnishing your home and counting the cost**   52

    FURNITURE   52
      Second-hand: sorting out the treasure from the trash   55
      The do-it-yourself approach   59
      Making the most of space   60

    FINANCE   61
      Budget accounts   61
      Going it alone   63
      Easy payment terms   64
      Money-saving ideas   64
      Keeping warm economically   66
      Sharing the costs   68
      Moonlighting   69
      Dealing with crises   70

6. **Decorating and do-it-yourself guide**   73

    DECORATING   73
      Creating illusions   74
      Working out quantity and quality   75
      Preparations for decorating   76
      Tools and techniques for painting   78
      Tools and techniques for wallpapering   81

    DOING IT YOURSELF   85
      Broken window   85
      Sticking doors or windows   89
      Faulty floorboards   90
      Weathered mortar   92
      Leaking tap   93
      Running overflow   94
      Blocked sink, basin or bath   95
      Leaking guttering or drainpipes   97
      Ill-fitting window frames   98
      Peeling window frames   98
      Cracks and holes in plaster   99
      Wall fixings   101
      Curtains   102
      Shelving   102

        Laying floor coverings   103
        Wiring a plug   105

7.   **Gardening and other hobbies**   109

       OUTDOOR GARDENING   109
         Flora   111
         Planning a garden   111
         Planting a herb garden   112
         Window-boxes   114

       INDOOR GARDENING   115

       MORE HOME HOBBIES   116
         Rug making   117
         Upholstery   118
         Beer and wine making   118
         Music   119
         And to conclude   120

Introduction

Setting up home for the first time is an exciting challenge in anyone's book. How well you meet that challenge is going to depend on your stamina, resourcefulness, and the advice you receive. Becoming a property owner isn't just about acquiring bricks and mortar; having a place of your own is inevitably going to bring big changes to virtually every part of your life. This book aims to be your guide, to answer questions, and to suggest a few you may not have thought of.

To begin with, how do you set about finding the home of your dreams? It's not always easy, especially if you are planning to settle in a new area and so are trying to find a suitable neighbourhood as well. Once you have located a few likely looking properties, what are the points to look for when the owners take you round?

When the search is over and you have found a house or flat you want to buy, the actual business of making it yours involves solicitors and a building society or bank, as well as a surveyor. It can all seem very confusing, but it needn't be. This book takes you through the home-buying process and suggests ways to arrange the move and establish yourself in your new home and area. Have you considered any money-saving ideas to furnish your house or flat and make ends meet? What about decorating and new hobbies?

There's also the emotional aspect of home ownership. Independence can sometimes be very lonely. It's vital that you know how to cope, by looking at the new opportunities open to you. On the other hand, there may be new commitments to either husband or wife, boyfriend or girlfriend, now that you are sharing a home together.

Does it all begin to sound rather daunting? It needn't be.

2 · *Setting up Home*

With a little forethought and care, setting up a home of your own can be one of the most exciting and rewarding times of your life. In the end you may well feel that you have achieved far more than just putting a roof over your head.

1
Finding and buying your new home

Among the millions of dwellings you could buy, ranging from the small flat to the grandest country mansion, there is one that is just right for you. The difficult part is actually finding it.

Househunting is a minefield fraught with danger. After all, it's not just a home you're looking for but also all that goes with it: the area, the neighbours and the local amenities. A des. res. of your dreams can become a nightmare if you don't make sure you know as much as possible before committing yourself to signing on the dotted line. After all, buying a house or a flat is going to be the biggest financial decision you have ever had to make, so you must get it right first time! This means not rushing into the very first property that takes your fancy. If you do, it could be a very costly mistake which you'll regret for years. Having said that, house-hunting can also be fun, you learn a lot as you go along, and after seeing a number of properties you'll have a far clearer idea of what you can and can't afford.

Houses and flats are expensive, and you must be realistic about how much money you can raise and how far it will go in the area in which you want to live. What would buy a comfortable detached house with garden and garage in one part of the country might be only just enough for a small flat in another. London and the south-east are notoriously expensive, and prices there can come as quite a shock if you have been living in the north or in parts of the Midlands. Perhaps you may have to work out a balance between what you want and what you can afford, but settling for second-best doesn't mean putting up with third-rate. The most important thing is to find a home which will suit you and your lifestyle.

A good way to begin is to jot down on paper the features you want in your new home. For example, if entertaining is important to you, then so would be a good-sized kitchen and dining area. On the other hand, if rustling up a tin of baked beans is stretching your culinary skills to the limit, something smaller would obviously do. What about a garden? Do you like gardening or are you happy with a window-box? Gardens can be attractive and wonderful to sit in during hot summer days, but they take a lot of looking after. Most modern houses these days have only a tiny garden, whereas older properties can have quite extensive ones.

Decide how many bedrooms you need. Even if you'll be living alone, three bedrooms aren't too many since the smallest one can become a study or hobbies room. If there are two of you living together a third bedroom is even more important, since there are bound to be times when you'll want to escape to peace and quiet for a while. Consider whether or not you want an open fire. Many modern houses don't have chimneys, and building one later would be prohibitively expensive.

Many people buying flats don't want to live in the basement or on the ground floor because of the reduced security. Blocks of flats are generally safer from unwelcome visitors if there is some kind of electronically operated front door.

You must also decide how much work you're prepared to do on the house or flat once you've bought it. Older properties invariably need work carrying out, and if this is not for you, confine yourself to looking at modern properties. However, rooms in newer houses are likely to be smaller.

Be as flexible as possible and be prepared to compromise. It's unlikely that you'll find exactly what you are looking for, so decide on the features that will be the cornerstone of your happiness. It's going to be a long slog before you can move, but if care is taken along the way, it should be well worth it.

Finding the right area

House buying is made much easier if you already know the area in which you want to live. If you're already part of the community it's easier still, because the chances are you'll know some of your future neighbours. Buying in the same street as relatives or friends has pluses as well as minuses. On the one hand there's always someone close by to water the plants and feed the pets if you go away for a few days. They will also be able to keep an eye on the property for you. On the other hand those same eyes may also watch you a bit too closely for comfort. Quite possibly you don't want your comings and goings monitored and broadcast around the family! But the advantages will probably outweigh the disadvantages, because it's never easy settling into an area and feeling part of the community.

The process is even more difficult when you move to another part of the country which you know little about and where everyone is a stranger. Choosing the area is difficult enough; choosing the property itself is even more daunting. To begin with it's a mass of unfamiliar streets and landmarks, but don't be put off – eventually you'll be able to call it home.

If you're moving to a strange town or city because of a new job, why not ring one of your future colleagues for advice? Local knowledge is invaluable, and could save you enormous amounts of time. Find out about property prices by buying a copy of the local paper and getting your name on estate agents' mailing lists. Tell the agents what you're looking for and what your price range is. You can then expect to be inundated with stacks of house particulars, most of which you'll probably throw in the bin as being completely unsuitable. But among them might be the property you're looking for.

Most estate agents send out fairly detailed particulars of the properties they have for sale. Usually there's a photograph and a description of each room with its measurements. The details are full of jargon. A house with 'potential' often requires considerable expenditure before it's fit to live in. 'Close to shops' can mean sandwiched between a newsagent and a Chinese takeaway. The particulars will highlight the property's features – central heating for instance – but don't expect to be told about the rising damp or the leaking roof. Estate agents want to sell the property as quickly as possible, and they are famous for exaggeration. 'A good-sized garden' is a matter of opinion, and words like 'character' and 'charming' crop up frequently.

Visit the area yourself and invest in a street guide. If you have a car, drive around and look out for home-made 'For Sale' signs. It might be worth putting your own advertisement in the paper saying exactly what you are looking for. Look at the local amenities: shops, parks, schools and public transport. Ask yourself whether you would be able to get to work easily, and most important of all, ask yourself whether you would enjoy living there. If not, look somewhere else.

The big city is not everyone's cup of tea, but usually it's convenient. Small towns and villages are often more attractive, but do they have the things you need? If you enjoy going out in the evenings to the theatre or cinema, village life can be dull to say the least. A place in the country might look ideal in summer, but try to imagine it in winter when your car won't start and the only bus runs long after you should be at work. A place on a city's perimeter might be a compromise. It would be easy enough to enjoy the shops and nightlife, but also easy enough to get out into the country at weekends.

It is no exaggeration to say that a neighbourhood can dramatically change its character along the length of one street, or from one street to the next. This is particularly true in urban areas. Don't, therefore, make a decision based purely on first impressions; do a little detective work as well. Find out about the area from someone who hasn't got a vested interest in whether you buy or not. Estate agents are hardly likely to tell you about an area's bad points – after all, they want the sale to go through so that they can collect their commission. The local paper is again invaluable here. It will give you an idea of the character of the area and an insight into its problems. Read about pressure groups concerned with problems which you had no idea existed in the area in which you want to buy. You could even go along to the paper's offices and discuss any specific points with the editor or one of the reporters.

The police station could also be worth a visit. Arrange to speak to the beat bobby who would patrol your road. You are not asking for a blow-by-blow account of people's criminal records, just an indication of the level of crime on his or her beat. If it's a multiracial area, you'll want to know of any tension that exists in the community. Another port of call might be the council offices. They'll be able to tell you of any major plans in the pipeline, although if you do decide to buy, it would be up to your solicitor to find out about plans directly affecting your property. In a smaller community like a village, the clerk to the parish council could be invaluable. Also, look at the noticeboards in the shop or church to find out about activities which go on. The village pub could also be the ideal place to pick up local gossip!

All this helps to build up a picture of the area in which you're interested, and will help you to decide whether it's a place where you would be able to fit in. If you have any doubts, remember that it is still early days and you can change your mind at any time.

Paying a visit

Once you have found a property which you think may be suitable, then the next step is actually to see inside. If you have to travel a long way to get there, perhaps arrange to see several properties in the course of a day. Some you'll be able to rule out straightaway, others may seem attractive, while perhaps one is just what you want. Most 'For Sale' boards have 'Viewing By Appointment' on them, so you'll have to fix up a time with the estate agent. The property may even be empty, in which case you'll have to arrange to meet the agent there. Some properties are sold privately; the home-made 'For Sale' signs make these obvious. Often, you can simply knock at the door and ask to be shown round, but again you may have to make an appointment.

Most people feel terribly embarrassed when they're given a conducted tour of someone else's home. As a result, they quickly step from room to room and are left with just a fleeting glimpse of the property's features – or the lack of them. Steel yourself! If you're seriously interested in buying, you'll want to know everything about the house and not just the glossy details in the estate agent's blurb. You'll do yourself no favours if you spend just a couple of minutes inside because you feel awkward abut examining someone else's bedroom or bathroom. After all, estate agents won't tell you about a house's bad points, and the seller will want to avoid mentioning them. So it's up to you to ask the right questions and get satisfactory answers. To make it easier, take along a list of things to look out for – and once inside, be thorough.

Of course, you won't be made welcome if you bring along a magnifying glass and penknife with which to dig out samples of the woodwork, but you can use your eyes to make sure doors and windows open as they should and the paintwork on the windowsills isn't peeling too badly. Oldstyle electrical switches and points indicate old wiring, and that could be a major expense for you. Don't be put off by awful wallpaper or colour schemes; these can easily be changed at minimum cost. More important are the fundamentals: is the house in generally good condition and dry inside?

If a musty smell greets you when you step inside, suspect a problem with damp. Peeling wallpaper and damp patches might confirm such suspicions. Damp may occur on the floor and ceiling just as much as on walls, and can be caused by both internal and external water sources. Some damp problems are relatively cheap and easy to fix; however, putting in a new damp course is expensive as it involves stripping off plaster. So if you don't want the expense or hassle, perhaps the house won't do after all. Remember to be suspicious of new paintwork and wallpaper. Ask yourself what it is hiding underneath.

Look at how secure the house is. Are there mortice locks on the doors leading outside, and are there any locks on the windows? If there is a burglar alarm system, ask the owner to demonstrate it. Don't assume anything works until it's been proven. Turn on the taps both upstairs and downstairs to check the water pressure, and see whether there is plumbing for a washing machine. Look at the heating system and ask about the central heating boiler if there is one. An old, inefficient boiler might need replacing – more expense for you. If it looks reasonably new, ask about any guarantees which might still be in force. Make sure the house hasn't got any cold spots, and ask about lagging to pipes and about insulation in the roof.

Once you have seen around inside, have a look outside. Work out which way the house faces. Having the main windows on the south side is best, because then the house gets the maximum amount of sunshine. Look at the roof for signs of slipping tiles. Inspect the guttering. Leaks here could show up by stains on the brickwork and damp patches inside the house. Look at the doors and windows to see if they are in good order. Has the house been generally well-maintained, or is it run down (fig. 1)?

If there isn't a garage and you have a car, check that there is somewhere to park it. Also, pay particular attention to the surrounding properties. Do they overlook the house or garden? The state of the garden next door might give you an indication of the kind of neighbours to expect. You could always ask about the neighbours, but don't expect an honest reply if they're the kind who've caused nothing but trouble. Who knows? That may be the reason the house is for sale.

Wander up and down the street outside to spot any potential nuisances. A pub close by could be a bonus, but at closing time the slamming of car doors might disturb you. A disused garage or workshop might look innocent enough, but who's to say the owner might not start up a

10 · *Setting up Home*

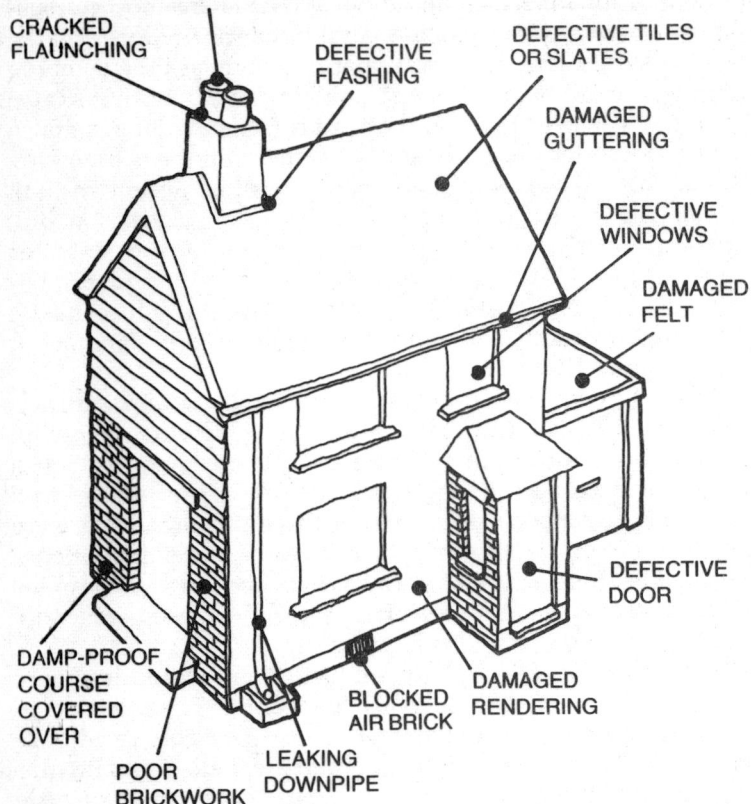

Fig 1

noisy business there. A church hall or community centre is another potential hazard: all quiet during the day, but at night it comes alive with loud music. It's often a good idea to pay several visits at different times of the day to get a feel of the kind of area it is. Be suspicious if you want to view a property and the owners claim the only convenient time is a Sunday morning when all is quiet and peaceful – it may not always be like that!

Of course, at this stage you're not committed to buying. There's a long way to go yet and plenty of opportunity to change your mind. But the more you find out for yourself now, the more you reduce the risk of disappointment later on. Whatever you do, don't rush into buying. Remember, there are millions of other homes and one of them could be far more suitable. But if this is the house or flat you want, lose no time in setting the wheels in motion. There is always the chance that someone else may come along and buy it instead.

The home-buying process

Actually buying a property involves you with estate agents, solicitors, surveyors and, last but not least, a building society or bank. It's a complicated process and can take anything from a month to three months to complete. You should have already been thinking about getting a mortgage, and may even have a provisional offer of one. At one time it used to be very difficult borrowing money to buy your own home. Even if you had been saving regularly with a building society, you might still have had to join a queue before your turn came up to be considered. Nowadays, it's a different matter entirely. Banks have branched out into lending money for homes and they compete fiercely with the traditional lender, the building society. Sometimes it seems as if banks and the various building societies are fighting each other for the privilege of lending you money – a nice position for a home buyer to be in.

If you have a building society account, it makes sense to go along to see your branch manager. Usually he or she will be able to agree in principle to lending you the money, provided the house or flat you choose is worth what you intend to borrow. Or you can go along to your bank manager and he or she might consider your request.

If you don't have a building society account, the estate

agent dealing with the property might be able to help. They have many contacts with building societies and will act as a go-between in finding a mortgage. Alternatively, there are mortgage brokers who specialise in linking prospective borrowers with building societies. Should none of this appeal to you, then your solicitor might be able to help. Provided you are in work, getting a mortgage should not be a problem.

Setting the wheels in motion

The first move is to make an offer for the house or flat you want to buy. The estate agent's details will have an asking price for the property. Buying a house or flat is not like buying something in a shop; a certain amount of haggling is usual, so don't immediately offer the exact amount that is being asked. You can probably put in an offer several thousand pounds below the asking price, but be prepared to increase it if it's not acceptable. The offer should be written down and sent to the estate agent, who will contact the owner on your behalf and advise him or her. Make the offer 'subject to contract', which means that it is not in any way binding and can be withdrawn at any time.

As a first-time buyer, you won't be involved in a 'chain': you don't have a house to sell and so you're not waiting on someone else to buy before you can get things moving. If the person selling to you, the 'vendor', is anxious to buy another house, being a first-time buyer is a positive advantage because it means there shouldn't be any unnecessary delays. This is one reason why a lower offer from you might be acceptable to the vendor. There might, however, be some toing and froing as the vendor tries to get you to increase your offer. A certain amount of brinkmanship is also involved, but hopefully you'll arrive at a price acceptable to you both. The next stage is to put the matter in the hands of your solicitor and formally apply for a mortgage.

Mortgages

Now you will know exactly how much you need to borrow, taking into account any improvements you will wish to make straightaway to the property. There are no hard and fast rules about the amount you will be lent, but it does depend on your age, your job, the property you're buying and the area it's in. Generally though, it's three times your annual income if you're buying on your own. For two people, whether they are married or not, it's three times one income (the largest) plus the annual income of the other. Remember, if you are intending to live together, the bank or building society will expect you to buy together. This applies even if only one of the partners is working.

First-time buyers can apply for a 100 per cent mortgage, in other words you can apply to borrow the whole amount that the property costs. But some banks and societies will expect you to put down some cash yourself, perhaps 5 or 10 per cent. Borrow as much as you can afford to, and as much as the bank or society is willing to lend you. Any savings of your own are best kept for carpets and curtains and the hundred and one other expenses which are involved when you move house. Having a phone put in, connecting up the cooker, not to mention the physical cost of moving your possessions, are just some of the expenses you'll have to meet. In any case, mortgages are a cheap way of borrowing money and qualify for tax relief.

Mortgage Tax Relief, known as MIRAS, is available to all first-time property buyers for up to £30,000 per dwelling. This means that a married couple or two people living together are only eligible for £30,000 tax relief between them. However, if you are purchasing a self-contained flat in a house which has been divided into separate living spaces, each unit or dwelling is entitled to the full £30,000 relief. Mortgage tax relief is deducted at source by the bank or society, so if you wish to apply for it you must ask the manager who is granting the mortgage for the appropriate forms.

Deciding how much to borrow is one problem. Deciding on the kind of mortgage is another. The two particularly suited for first-time buyers are 'repayment' and 'endowment'. A repayment mortgage involves borrowing a lump sum over a set number of years, anything from 20 to 35. Each month you pay an amount to the bank or building society, partly to pay off the interest and partly to pay off the lump sum. In the early years of the mortgage, most of the monthly payments are taken up with paying the interest. But as the years go by, the balance shifts so you're paying off only a little interest and a larger slice of the capital sum. There is no insurance policy automatically attached to a mortgage of this kind, but most banks and building societies would encourage you to take out some form of protection in case of redundancy or even death.

With an endowment mortgage, the capital and interest are treated separately. You borrow the capital sum in the same way, but each month you only pay off the interest on it. At the same time, you take out an endowment assurance policy. You pay into the policy each month as well, and the idea is that when it matures there will be enough money to pay off the entire capital sum in one go. If you're lucky, there'll also be some money left over which would be yours, tax free. One advantage of endowment policies is that they can be transferred from one property to another when you move. Endowment policies are generally slightly more expensive than repayment mortgages.

With both forms of mortgage, the amount you pay back each month can vary as interest rates go up and down. Be aware of these fluctuations when you decide how much you want to borrow.

The role of the solicitor

You will need a solicitor to do the 'conveyancing', the actual legal process of buying. It is possible to do it yourself and there are books on the subject, but it's generally regarded as unwise. Your bank or society may insist that a solicitor acts for you. If you don't know one, ask around among friends and relatives for a recommendation, or go to the Citizens' Advice Bureau. There's nothing to stop you shopping around for the best quote because legal fees, like everything else, are expensive.

A solicitor's job is to do the donkey work for you, look after your interests, and generally make sure you are not being taken for a ride. There's a lot of mystique about conveyancing, but in practice it involves the solicitor writing a lot of letters.

The vendor's solicitor will send yours a draft contract of sale. He or she will have to go through this very carefully and raise any 'pre-contract enquiries'. These generally consist of establishing who owns the boundary walls, what rights anybody else has over the property, where the drains run, and so on. Your solicitor will also carry out a 'search', which involves finding out whether any planning schemes with the local authority might affect the property. These could be anything from a new block of flats going up next door, providing a view into your bedroom, to a massive new road scheme cutting across your front garden.

The advantage of employing a solicitor rather than doing it yourself is that if he or she fails to do the job properly, you can sue. Allow about a month for the solicitor to make his or her enquiries.

The bank or building society will send a surveyor round to see the house or flat. This is purely for their benefit, to make sure the property is worth the money you intend spending on it. You will have to pay for this. If you want a survey which includes advice, you can ask for a more detailed one to be carried out. Alternatively, you can commission a surveyor yourself. The simplest way is to go to another firm of estate agents and ask someone there to look over the house on your behalf. You can also phone the Royal Institution of Chartered Surveyors in London (01-222 7000) for the name of someone local.

Your surveyor will look carefully at every room, as well as

the outside of the house, and will prepare a report for you. He or she will also give you an estimate of the property's value. If the surveyor suspects major problems like damp or dry rot, he or she will recommend a specialist survey. Far better to find out what is wrong now, rather than later when you are in residence. If there are major problems, the building society may insist you get them put right as a condition of your mortgage. You can use the surveyor's report as a lever to push the price of the property down.

Once the solicitor has reported to you that everything is in order, the bank or building society has agreed to lend you the money, and the surveyor hasn't been found anything seriously wrong with the house, you are then in a position to exchange contracts. This involves signing the contract of sale, signing the mortgage agreement, and agreeing with the vendor on a 'completion' date, the time when you actually take over the property.

When all that is done, you will be a homeowner. It's been a long hard slog with, no doubt, frustrations along the way. But at least you know exactly what you are buying and what its potential is. If you can make the monthly mortgage payments without too much difficulty, the future should be looking bright. It's been tough, but it will be worth it as you move into a home of your own.

2
Moving day and security for the home

MOVING

Setting up home can be a tremendous upheaval, both physically and emotionally. In fact, buying a home and moving is judged to be as stressful as getting married or having a baby. The actual move involves organising the packing and transport, and probably a spring-clean before unloading can begin. Although some new owners complete their move over a weekend or even a day, the sensible approach is to try and take a holiday from work while you're settling in.

Warn your employers well in advance that you're involved in a property sale and would like some time off in the near future. Try to avoid giving a specific date until you know for sure when the keys are going to be handed over. It's wise to be as flexible as possible, in case there's an unforeseen hitch which holds up completion. Consider how frustrating it would be if the move was postponed and you couldn't adjust your holiday accordingly.

In the weeks leading up to the moving date, begin building up a stockpile of old newspapers, wrapping paper, and of course cardboard boxes. Tea chests are a great asset but not always easy to find and there is usually a small charge.

While working out what you need for the move, spare a thought for your own well-being. Dashing around and skipping meals will leave you feeling tired and hardly in a fit state to meet the challenge of setting up a new home. Regard yourself as an athlete in training, who has to eat well to build up stamina. If you feel you might not last the course, ask either your doctor or pharmacist for advice on taking any vitamin or iron supplements.

Taking the strain out of packing

Where you are moving to, and who is going to help, ought to have some bearing on how you pack. Small boxes are a must if home sweet home is a sixth-floor flat with no lift and the helpers are high on enthusiasm but low on muscle power. The ideal container for packing glasses is a box which has previously been used to transport wine bottles. The cardboard partitions inside the box will stop the glasses rolling around in transit. Soft furnishings, such as cushions or small rugs, can be stuffed down the sides of boxes to protect large breakable items. Wrap strips of cardboard around table legs and furniture corners to guard against scrapes. Write on every box what's inside. If you don't, you'll never remember which one is which once they've been jumbled up.

Since it's highly unlikely that everything is going to be unpacked on the first day, work out a packing programme. What will be needed in the first hours should be the last things packed. The obvious items are crockery and cutlery, bedlinen, toiletries and a change of clothes. Items of clothing can be transported in their drawers, as long as they don't prove too cumbersome.

Removal firms versus DIY

The easy option but the most expensive involves hiring a removal firm to come in, pack everything up and transport the lot to your new home. The big removal vans can comfortably take the entire contents of a house. Ring round several removal firms for quotes to see who can offer the best deal, and check that all the expenses, such as insurance, mileage and the men's labour, are included in the estimate. Always give the removal team precise instructions on how to reach their destination. Even if they are following the car, it's easy to get separated in a strange city. On the day of the move, if finding a parking space outside your home is going to be difficult, ask the local police if they will put cones along your frontage so that the removal van is able to park.

The alternative to hiring a removal firm is to drive a van yourself. The DIY approach is probably the more attractive option for people who are setting up home for the first time and haven't acquired much furniture. To be eligible, the driver must have a full and valid driving licence held for at least a year, so that puts the minimum age at 18-plus, and must have no serious endorsements. Both the 18-cwt transit van and the 35-cwt Luton can be driven on a normal driving licence.

Van hire is an extremely competitive market, so again ring round for the best quote. Firms which belong to the British Vehicle Rental and Leasing Association abide by a strict code of practice. Members must buy new models and run the smaller models for only three years. Local firms may be cheaper than some of the big national operators, but they can't always match the deals on offer, as with one-way hire, for instance. This is ideal for the long-distance move which can be completed in one journey.

Before signing the firm's lease agreement, ask whether the charge is worked out by mileage or at a day rate, although some companies operate a system which combines the two. Also, check on the insurance cover being provided, there could be a sting in the tail. Some firms stipulate the driver pays part of any accident repair bills, and your share could run into hundreds of pounds. One way to avoid such an expense is to take out a collision damage waiver policy which, as the name implies, protects the driver from any bills. Personal accident coverage is usually an optional extra but certainly worth considering. Finally, ask if the van hire firm operate their own call-out service or arrange for their customers to have temporary membership of a national breakdown organisation.

The driver must bear in mind that even though the vehicle is hired, the person at the wheel is held responsible for it roadworthy condition. Before leaving the forecourt, test the lights and indicators, make sure all the brakes are sound, and check that the tyre tread meets legal requirements.

Driving a transit van can seem rather a daunting prospect if your normal runabout is a small car. The key to making a smooth transition lies in learning to judge the width and length of the vehicle, and its manoeuvrability in relation to the lock on the wheel. Try motoring around a few quiet streets to gain confidence before loading up. The additional weight in the back will add momentum to the van when travelling at speed, so allow extra stopping distance between you and the car travelling in front.

The move

Seeing your new home stripped of all its furniture, pictures and carpets can be quite a shock. Rooms which might have appeared clean can look quite filthy when devoid of furnishings. The previous owners are under no obligation to leave their former home spotless. They are only obliged to uphold the terms of the sale agreed in the contract.

Splashing out on bin liners, cleaning equipment and detergents will be a worthwhile investment. If they aren't needed when moving in, they certainly will be once you start living in your new home. Bleach is very good for lifting ground-in stains on kitchen worktops etc., as well as killing germs. Detergent-based cleaners are effective in cutting through grease. When there's too much rubbish for the dustbin men to clear, either ring the council to find out where the nearest tip for domestic refuse is, or hire a skip. You will need permission from the local authority to site the skip in the road.

Family and friends usually rally round when help is required. The old saying 'Many hands make light work' certainly rings true when everyone is properly organised.

Draw up a plan of who does what before the move gets underway. Your scheme can be as simple as dividing people into two groups, the cleaners and the carriers. Once the mop brigade has finished, the furniture and boxes can be carried in. Use a colour-coding scheme so that everyone knows where things are supposed to go. Place different-coloured stickers on each door and mark items accordingly.

Don't forget to put together a special emergency box. Be prepared for little accidents and include a basic first-aid kit, as well as scissors, cord or string, screwdriver, hammer and an assortment of nails and screws for those odd jobs which need to be tackled immediately. Enclose a few light bulbs just in case the previous owners have taken theirs with them.

Rewarding refreshments

Providing food for your helpers can be a problem, especially if the cooker hasn't been installed yet. Paying a visit to the local fish and chip shop or takeaway is the easy answer, but they're not always conveniently situated around the corner. An easy alternative is to have a help-yourself picnic. Instead of preparing sandwiches, which invariably end up a soggy mess, let people make up their own. Buy several sticks of French bread and provide the fillings. A selection of cheeses, pâtés and slices of cold meat, followed by fresh fruit, should suffice and will keep well in a cooler box.

Hot food is easily cooked either out of doors or in a slow cooking pot. A barbecue can be as simple as a few stacked bricks with a grill resting on the top. Wrap jacket potatoes in silver foil and let them cook on the surface of the charcoal. The grill is then left free to sizzle sausages. A slow cooking pot uses about the same amount of electricity as a light bulb and slowly cooks the food in its own juices or in stock. Most recipes simply require an odd stir, otherwise forget about it until serving-up time.

In the rush, don't forget to notify the gas and electricity boards of the date when you're taking possession. They'll send round their officials to read the meters and reconnect supplies. It is sometimes possible to take over the telephone number of your new home if the previous owners are agreeable and British Telecom are informed. But the former owners may decide to take their number with them if they're moving only a short distance.

SECURITY

It might seem a little premature to be looking at security just as you're settling in, but fixing new locks and so on tends to be one of those jobs which are easy to put off and put off – until it's too late. Police figures show that burglars often pay a visit after someone has just moved in. The burglar gambles that the neighbours will be only vaguely aware of people carrying boxes around. But this time, they're being taken out instead of in.

To detect how accessible your new home is to an intruder, try thinking like a thief. You want to get in, so how would you go about it without being spotted? Perhaps around the back, if the windows are on a simple latch. Even better if they are next to a drainpipe or overlook a flat roof. Glass panels in French windows are easily smashed. All the burglar probably then has to do is turn the key left in the lock or twist the knob on a simple nightlatch lock.

Most burglaries are committed by the opportunist thief: if the break-in looks easy, then the thief will have a go. On the shopping list will be the TV, video, music centre, in fact most of the electrical goods lying around. The after-effects of a burglary can be long lasting. After the stolen items have been replaced, the feelings of violation may still linger.

The police insist that many burglaries could be prevented if only people would carry out the basics and fit security locks to windows and doors. Before spending any money, contact the Crime Prevention Officer at your local police station. Many CPOs make their calls in plain clothes to avoid attracting attention and causing embarrassment. They will point out where a burglar could gain entry, even highlight problems you might not have thought of such as louvre windows. The glass slate at the top of these can be easily removed. The space might be too small for an adult to climb through, but not for a child who then opens the door and lets in his or her accomplice. A cheap remedy is to glue the slats in place with an epoxy resin adhesive, although there are specially designed locks available.

Which lock to choose

The choice of security locks for doors and windows is vast, but there are two main types, mortice locks and rim locks. Mortice locks are embedded in the wood while rim locks rest on top. A lock, however, is only as good as the surface which holds it. Spending a fortune on various locks won't improve your security if the wood to which you attach them is rotten or too thin. The mortice is designed to enhance the strength of the timber, but it will not be very effective if, in fitting the mortice, too much wood is taken out. A better choice then would be a rim lock, which is screwed on.

Mortice locks which meet specifications laid down by the British Standards Institution display the BS kitemark. The standard (BS 3621) stipulates a lock must have at least five levers, which means it is virtually impossible to pick; it must also have hardened plates or rollers to resist drilling, 1,000 key variations, and a deadlock action so that once shut it can't be drawn back without a key. When choosing a rim lock, look for ones which also have an automatic deadlock action, concealed screw heads, and a lockable latch handle to prevent the burglar flicking off the latch if he or she has pushed his or her hand through the glass.

Replacing an old mortice lock with a new one of the same size shouldn't be too difficult: the holes and recess are already there. Rim locks are generally easier to fit than mortice locks. They are screwed into place, but obviously the alignment has to be spot on. Chain locks on doors are also easy to install. Again, it's just a matter of aligning the chain holder and sliding case. Door viewers can give up to a 160° angle of vision and are fitted by drilling a hole through the door. For extra protection, bolts can be fitted to both doors and windows. There are many types of these.

If your carpentry skills aren't up to such detailed work, ask the Crime Protection Officer to recommend a handyman who can do the job.

Putting up window stickers, which advertise the fact that valuables inside carry identification marks, is another effective deterrent. A thief will think twice about stealing items carrying the owner's postcode in ultraviolet ink. The police put all recovered stolen property under special lights to see if it has been marked in this way. They also urge owners to keep a record of serial numbers on any electrical goods.

Still at the cheaper end of the market are timer switches for lights. Police figures show that many burglaries occur at dusk before the owner comes home from work. Lights shining in an upstairs room or in the sitting-room give the impression that someone is at home. Even if the burglar has been watching the house and knows everyone is out, there is a better chance he or she will be spotted against a lighted background than a darkened window.

Some householders not only have a light timer fitted but also attach a few lights outside their home, often in the guise of decorative lanterns. Running costs can be kept to a minimum by installing light bulbs which use less electricity than the ordinary household variety, or by connecting a photocell controller to switch the lights on at dusk and off at dawn.

Burglar alarms are considered by many to be the ultimate deterrent against a break-in. The alarm-bell systems usually include: magnetic door and window contacts, which set off the alarm when opened; space detectors, often sited by doorways and activated if someone breaks their beam; pressure pads; an external bell; panic buttons, active even when the system is switched off; and finally the control panel. The Crime Prevention Officer will be able to recommend several companies who may also belong to the NSCIA, which stands for the National Supervisory Council for Intruder Alarms. Members are bound by a code of conduct which stipulates that they must provide an all-year-round service 24 hours a day.

When a silent burglar alarm is triggered, a message is automatically sent along the telephone line to a monitoring station. The controller on duty calls the police. This type of system is more expensive, because of the rental charges and maintenance of the dialler.

Strong locks, timer switches and burglar alarms are effective weapons in the fight against crime. If you don't use them you could be the next victim.

3
Settling in and getting on with the neighbours

As the move ends, the settling-in period begins. It might be some time before your new flat or house and the area start to feel like home. How long it takes is going to depend on you and your attitude.

Decorating every room is an expensive way to obliterate all signs of the previous owners, and not everyone has the money or time to carry out such a cosmetic overhaul. It is often better actually to live in a new home for a while and get the feel of the place before deciding on any painting projects. When cash is tight, consider cheaper alternatives which will go some way to making home seem a little more homely, at least for the first few months.

Why not plan a paper cover-up and plaster the walls with posters and pictures? Decorate naked light bulbs with paper lampshades. Plain ones can be livened up by drawing on your own design. Curtains go a long way to creating a new look. If the previous owners have taken all of theirs, this will be a number one priority. Curtains can be bought ready-made or be made to measure. If you decide to make them yourself, make sure you allow plenty of material for the folds, half as much again as the width of the window will be ample. Let them hang at least six inches below the window frame to ensure they keep out draughts. Blinds are fairly inexpensive and easy to put up. They can add an interesting dash of colour to a room.

Now you are in residence, it is important that you let the outside world know. There is a long list of people you need to inform about your new address, quite apart from friends and family. Your bank, credit card companies, the premium bond office, passport office, motoring organisation and the car licensing centre at Swansea are among the most important people who need to know you have moved. Your employers must also be informed. You might consider having some change of address cards printed. If you don't already know your postcode, find out by checking with the post office.

You will also have to start paying rates or community charge, so tell the local council and the water authority. If you don't, they'll catch up with you eventually and then the bill will be even larger. Get yourself on the electoral roll, too, so that you can take part in elections. The council will have a special electoral roll department which you should contact.

The previous occupants may have made arrangements with the post office to have their mail forwarded. If they haven't, and you get inundated with their post, simply write on the envelopes 'not known at this address' and deposit them in the nearest post box.

Gas and electricity meters should be read on the day you move in, so that you don't end up paying for somebody else's heat and light. Look in the phone book under Gas or Electricity and ask for a meter reader to call.

Getting the job done

If there are major jobs to be tackled which you don't feel confident about doing yourself, you'll have to call in a local tradesman. This is another area fraught with danger, because there are so many cowboy outfits which may not do the job well but which will still charge you the earth. Even if you don't need anything doing immediately, it is always a good idea to have a list of reliable people you can call on in emergencies. Once again, personal recommendation is best but not always possible.

If no one can suggest a good plumber or electrician, turn to the Yellow Pages or a local directory. Look for plumbers who advertise that they are members of the Institute of Plumbing and who therefore will abide by its strict code of conduct. Anyone can call him- or herself a plumber, but not everyone can become a member of the Institute.

Electricians ought to be members of either the Electrical Contractors' Association or the National Inspection Council for Electrical Installation Contracting. Both organisations are there to guard the good name of qualified electricians and keep the cowboys at bay.

General handymen are a different kettle of fish. They have no trade organisation, and to find a good one is purely a matter of luck. If you do hire someone, don't let him or her start any job before giving you an estimate of the final bill.

As soon as you move into a new home, you should also get on the lists of a doctor and dentist. The post office will have the names and addresses of local GPs and dental surgeons. It is also worth knowing who your local councillor is and the name of your MP, in case you ever have the kind of problem which only they can solve. The library or council office will provide you with their names and telephone numbers.

So much for inside the home, but you will also find it useful to know which are the best local shops, where the launderette is, and so on. Don't hesitate to introduce yourself to the local butcher and baker. You are far more likely to get what you want if you actually know them and they can look on you as a regular customer. Decide whether you want milk delivered, and if so waylay the milkman one morning. Have your newspapers delivered if an early morning cuppa isn't the same without a paper to read. After all, this is your home and the more you can do to make it feel comfortable, the happier you'll be.

Neighbours

Neighbours are often the key to feeling happy and contented in your own home. After all, it is comforting to know that there are people close by to whom you can turn in a crisis – even if that crisis is simply running out of sugar! But don't take good neighbours for granted; be prepared to do a little spadework to cultivate a good relationship.

As soon as you move in, or even before, go around next door and introduce yourself. The onus really is on you. You may feel shy and be sitting at home hoping the neighbours will take the initiative and call, but they may be shy, too, and hoping you'll make the first move. So knock on the door, make yourself known, and take it from there. They might be astonished that anyone should think of doing such a thing, and therefore be far more grateful for it.

It can't be emphasised too strongly how important it is to get on with the folk next door. They can make your life heaven or hell.

Many of the complaints handled by the Citizens' Advice Bureaux are about neighbourly squabbles, and some of them can be incredibly petty. Good relations are cemented by a little understanding. If you don't want your neighbour to play loud music at night, don't do it yourself. You may be surprised how far sound travels in the wee small hours of the morning.

If there is a problem, it's best to get it sorted out as soon as possible and prevent any unpleasantness later. A quiet word at the time is better than banging on the wall in frustration when it has all got too much to bear. Most people, after all, are reasonable and probably don't realise they are causing a nuisance. Look at your own lifestyle. Are you the best person in the world to live next door to?

Many neighbourly disputes flourish in the garden. The arguments are usually over simple things like overhanging branches or trees and shrubs which block out light. Half an hour's pruning could defuse the situation. Pets rampaging through the garden aren't usually welcome unless they're your own, and smelly refuse piling up in a corner is bound to cause offence sooner or later. Balls being constantly kicked into your garden can be a nuisance. There isn't much you can do about it, though, except to appeal to your neighbour's better nature. You are not allowed by law to confiscate the ball; you have to give it back or leave it where it is. But your neighbour or the children responsible aren't allowed to clamber into your garden to get it back, so stalemate ensues unless understanding wins the day.

Perhaps the most common problem encountered by people living close to someone else is noise. There's nothing worse than the 'thump, thump' of music played too loud. If your neighbour won't see reason, you can contact the local council who may send an environmental health officer to monitor the noise level. If it is excessive, the council can prosecute. Chances are however, that when the environmental health officer actually arrives, the perpetrators will have gone out for the evening. As a last resort, you can take out a private prosecution. However, this is difficult, expensive and can destroy any hope of building a relationship with your neighbour. Tact and diplomacy are the best methods for dealing with a nuisance, so try them first before getting heavyhanded.

Solicitors often say that if a problem seems insoluble, the only way to guarantee dealing with it effectively is to move.

It is by no means certain that you will come across any of the problems mentioned in this chapter. With luck you won't. Most people recognise that living close to someone else requires a bit of give and take. So long as you are prepared to do your best, it is likely that your neighbour will do the same.

Open house or sanctuary

The first week or so in your new home will probably be taken up with the more pressing practical problems which need seeing to. But it is also a time to consider the role you want the house or flat to play in your life. Is it, for instance, a place you can withdraw to from the outside world, or will it be the centre of your social life? If the latter is the case, don't delay – ask friends round today! No one expects you to have everything in shipshape order within 24 hours of moving in. Simply invite friends and relations round for a drink one evening. They'll be anxious to find out how the move has gone, and will be interested to see the flat or house they have been hearing so much about. They'll be prepared to rough it, just as long as you are too.

On the other hand, you may not want people encroaching on your new found independence. It may have been one of the reasons why you wanted to branch out in the first place. A home can be your retreat from the hectic pace of life outside. You may prefer to spend your spare time making it as comfortable and homely as possible, a place where you can curl up in front of the television or stereo.

When deciding on decor and furniture, you should bear these points in mind. If you are intending to keep visitors out, a cosy armchair or two in the living-room will probably be all you need to sit on.

But whichever you decide, open house or sanctuary, the simple message is, start as you mean to go on. It's your home, so therefore it's what you want that counts.

Other visitors

Apart from those visitors you have invited to your new home, you are quite likely to receive a few uninvited ones. Some may be welcome, others probably won't be.

It is quite usual for the local parish priest to call on newcomers to an area, and he may be particularly welcome if you are a churchgoer. A representative of a local pressure group may also pay a visit in the hope of finding a new recruit to join the cause. Neither of these visitors, or anyone in a similar role is likely to put any pressure on you whatsoever. You may feel glad that they have taken the trouble to come and see you.

On the other hand, 'Sold' signs on 'For Sale' boards can act as a magnet to enterprising door-to-door salesmen with their smooth patter and apparently unbeatable offers for new home-owners. But don't rush into anything; many individuals have made a fortune selling various forms of home improvements by this method, at the home-owners' expense. The most notorious are the double-glazing salesmen who refuse to take no for an answer, and the cowboy builders who are only too ready to point out loose tiles or leaking guttering. Any Citizens' Advice Bureau has horror stories to tell of people pressurised into buying 'improvements' they never wanted or needed. If you are tempted to take up such an offer, at least make it clear you want some time to think it over. Then go to other firms for quotes which you can compare. The motto here is 'Pay in haste, repent at leisure'.

Building up a social life

To feel part of a community you were not brought up in can take years. This is particularly true in small villages, where someone who has been living there for up to 20 years can still be regarded as a newcomer. In cities, with their more fluid populations, it is far easier to claim some sort of identity with an area, although harder actually to get to know people. Because it's a slow, patient process, get started on building up some kind of social life straightaway.

Quite clearly, if you and a few of your work colleagues live in the same area, it is far easier to build up a new circle of friends. Lifelong friendships are often forged at work by the sheer necessity of rubbing shoulders with other people day in and day out. However, if your new home is in a new area where you know no one, building up a circle of friends is likely to be a much slower process.

You may want to get involved in local politics or societies – that is, groups of people who meet regularly and talk about the things which interest you. The best place to find out what's available is at the local library. Most libraries have a noticeboard which will list the times and places of the different group meetings. Having decided what you are interested in, go along and introduce yourself.

The parish priest has already been mentioned. But churches aren't simply about turning up for Sunday services, they are involved in many other activities. Details of these can usually be found on a noticeboard in the church itself.

Many people with newfound time on their hands want to use it to broaden their knowledge. Evening classes are the answer. Nowadays you can study anything from French GCSE level to car maintenance. The choice is huge, and it's up to you to pick one which you will enjoy and will be able to stick at during the long winter evenings ahead. Classes usually run from the autumn term onwards, with enrolment in September. Once again, the library will have details of what's on offer. Consider matching your course with your needs. Someone setting up home for the first time might find courses in practical woodwork more useful than learning a second language.

If sport is your idea of relaxation, get involved in a local club. Sports centres exist to bring people together, and many people consider working up a sweat one of the best ways to relax!

One other place which often acts as the focal point of a local community is the pub. Even in this more enlightened age, it is difficult if you are a single girl to go into a pub and feel comfortable, although it depends on the individual girl and on the pub itself. But pubs are useful places to get to know people in convivial surroundings, and when everyone tends to be in a more relaxed mood than at other times of the day. Many pubs run their own sports teams and outings, and you could even do a couple of nights a week behind the bar as a means of getting to know the regulars.

Whatever you decide, do it. If you don't get up and get involved in activities when you first move in, you probably won't ever make the effort; and that would be a pity for you and for the friends you otherwise would have made.

4
Relationships: coming to terms with living alone or in a new partnership

Home ownership doesn't just involve bricks and mortar, mortgages and bills. It is also about learning to live alone or about learning how to cope with a new relationship. How successful you are in the years to come may well depend on the pattern which develops in the first few months of moving in.

GOING SOLO

Your status has changed. Along with the keys to the front door came new responsibilities and, perhaps for the first time, independence from family and friends. Buying a house or flat is a milestone in most people's lives and, as with any major upheaval, is quite likely to trigger off a whole range of conflicting emotions. Instead of confidence, there's self-doubt. Even when the move has been eagerly anticipated, you may suddenly begin to question your own judgement. 'Have I done the right thing?' 'Can I cope?' 'Is it all going to be too much for me?'

The answer lies in supplying your own morale boosters and adopting a more positive attitude. Begin by regarding the building society or bank's mortgage offer as a vote of confidence in you. After all, they would hardly lend you the money if they didn't think you could meet the repayments. Be reassured that if millions of other people can buy their own home, then so can you. Don't lose sight of the reason why you wanted to buy in the first place. Were you fed up with living with your parents or paying rent to a landlord? Did you want to be independent and stand on your own two feet? What about all those things you wanted to do but were putting off until the day you had a place of your own? If you moved because of your job, remind yourself of the new opportunities opening up at work.

During the first few weeks, stand by to receive a barrage of advice from well-meaning family and friends. This may require you to enforce your right to privacy and insist on working out your problems for yourself. Don't lose your new-found independence by having a stream of unannounced visitors who arrive to 'see how you're getting on'. Gently insist on some prior warning, and make it clear that it is your home and you don't need checking up on.

If this is the first time you have lived on your own, you'll be surprised at the number of regular jobs that suddenly present themselves to be done. In the old days you may have been able to rely on someone else to do your washing and cooking, not to mention the cleaning and looking after such mundane items as the dustbin. These things are now up to you.

A little planning will now be necessary to make the best use of your time at home. It is better to shop in one big batch once a week rather than nipping round to the corner shop every time you feel peckish. Apart from anything else, shopping in bulk at a supermarket is very much cheaper than relying on the small shops that stay open late into the evening.

Don't let your dirty washing build up for weeks on end or it will soon develop into an unmanageable pile. Dealing with it is probably one of the less appealing jobs of the week, but it can't be put off indefinitely or you will wake one morning to discover you have nothing clean to wear. Of course, if you have a washing machine and tumble drier the problem is easily solved. Otherwise, it's likely to be a regular trip to the launderette.

Many people will have never been inside a launderette

until the day they start to live on their own. Although it is certainly a chore to trudge down there with your washing, it is also by far the best method of getting everything clean and dry in one go. It is a good idea to empty your pockets or purse of small change each night and put it to one side for the sole purpose of feeding the washers and driers. Nothing is more irritating than arriving at a launderette without adequate change, and quite often nearby shops are reluctant to convert your pound coins into 10p pieces. Some launderettes operate what is called a service wash: you can leave your dirty clothes in the morning and pick them up later, washed and dried. You will have to pay for this of course, but it is worth it if time is short.

Living on your own for the first time can bring on feelings of isolation and loneliness. The best way to counter this is by having something to do with your free time. The suggestions in the last chapter should help you get to know new people, but tackling jobs around the house or even taking up a new hobby may help to dispel the sensation of being locked in and lonely.

Entertaining and eating well

Having a place of your own opens up a whole new world of home-based entertainment. Perhaps for the first time, you have the opportunity to play host to family and friends with a meal or a party.

You can kill two birds with one stone by having some kind of decorating party. If there is a room which needs stripping or you have large areas to be painted, why not invite a few willing friends to join in? Suggest they come round in old clothes and bring a paintbrush and bottle. No one really minds sploshing paint about when in a convivial mood helped along by food and drink. Supply paper plates and plastic glasses and get your friends working! If you think their standards might not be as high as yours, let them concentrate on the vast expanses of wall and do the tricky little bits yourself later on. It is surprising how quickly major jobs can get done if everyone lends a hand. Call a halt before they get bored, or before the drinks affect their painting arms.

A more traditional house or flat-warming party provides a good opportunity to show off your new home. If you can arrange the party before the carpets are laid, so much the better. It won't matter then if wine and beer are splashed about a little too enthusiastically. Concentrate on supplying buffet-type food with plenty of French bread, cheese, quiches and neatly cut raw vegetables with a choice of dips. Your guests will provide most of the drink, but have a supply of fruit juices, cola and some tonic available.

If you want to push the boat out, plan a full-blown dinner party. It will need careful planning and preparation, especially if cooking facilities are limited. Choose recipes you are familiar with and know you can handle, a dinner party is not the best time to experiment with exotic dishes that look mouthwatering in the cookery book picture but can quite easily turn out to be a disaster. If facilities are limited, go for a ready-prepared sweet like gâteau or sorbet from a supermarket deep freeze, or simply put out a cheese board. It's surprising how expensive a dinner party can be. Although your guests will probably bring a bottle of the right stuff, you'll also be expected to serve drinks before the meal and quite possibly afterwards, as well as providing the food.

If you are planning to entertain after a day at work, a slow pot cooker might be the answer to your prayers. There are many different types on the market, all fairly reasonably priced. They work on the principle of cooking a casserole-type meal very slowly over a period of several hours. This means you can set it going before leaving the house for work, and when you get home in the evening everything will be done to perfection. They are very economical and the boast is that they use only a light bulb's worth of electricity. Slow pot cookers aren't designed simply for entertaining. They can be a very useful gadget for you at other times, too. Imagine coming home on a winter's evening, cold and tired from work, and being greeted with delicious smells from the slow pot.

Living on your own provides the opportunity to devise your own eating plan, concentrating on the foods you like and that will do you good. Now is the time to experiment. After all, there is only yourself to please.

There is a greater emphasis these days on healthy eating, and if you have not been used to doing the weekly shopping you may be surprised at the huge range of good food available. Supermarkets now recognise that there is a rapidly increasing market for foods that are low in additives and artificial flavours and high in fibre and natural vitamins. Some also stock a range of organically grown vegetables, those that have been produced without fertilisers and have not been sprayed with pesticides. They are more expensive, but many people consider the expense worth while.

Cooking, of course, isn't everyone's idea of fun. Takeaway shops thrive on such people. Although it's undoubtedly quick and easy to buy a ready-cooked and packaged meal, it doesn't make good nutritional sense to have one every night. But whichever way you choose to eat, make sure you do get at least one good meal a day. Lack of food makes you tired and irritable and can bring on depression. A good meal has the opposite effect and contributes to a general feeling of well-being.

Sharing with a lodger

Living on one's own isn't everyone's idea of fun, especially when previously used to the hustle and bustle of a busy household. It is possible to have company without the commitment of a relationship by taking in a lodger. If that doesn't appeal, well, you can always give house-room to a pet.

A spare bedroom gives you the option of having someone to share if living alone becomes unbearable or your salary isn't enough to pay the bills. Before setting the wheels in motion, check that there isn't a clause in the mortgage agreement forbidding you to rent out part of your home. There probably is, and if you go ahead without the bank or building society's permission you face losing your home if they ever find out.

Charging someone rent, even for a bedroom in your own home, makes you a landlord and the lodger a tenant with rights under the law. Even when there is no formal agreement between the two of you, the lodger cannot be evicted on a whim. A month's notice would be a fair warning, but if the lodger decides to stay put, there's little that you can do without resorting to the courts. Signing a shorthold tenancy agreement, which means the contract to share lasts for at least one year but not more than four, offers some protection. It is best to seek the advice of a solicitor in all cases, or at the very least use a standard printed contract available at law stationers.

When the primary reason for wanting a lodger is for companionship rather than for the financial advantages, the thought of a formal contract can seem too businesslike. But a legal agreement may be your only protection, and might offer some reassurance to your lodger. Once the document has been signed, it need never be mentioned again. No one is suggesting it should be nailed to the bedroom door.

Probably the best kind of lodger is someone already known to you. The pitfall here is that you never really know a person until you actually live in the same house together. Someone whom you have always considered to be 'respectable' may turn out to have very antisocial habits at home! However, the advantage with someone you know is that at least you can have a full and frank exchange of views before he or she moves in. This is the time to lay down a few basic ground rules and discover areas of disagreement before actually committing yourself.

Simple matters like not allowing dirty pots and pans to gather for days on the draining board might seem trivial, but to people who like to keep a clean and orderly house they take on far greater importance.

Agree that the washing of dirty crockery is done by the person who has used them. Make it clear that you expect your lodger to play a full part in keeping the house or flat clean and tidy – and that includes the bathroom and loo. You could agree to take it in turns to do a big clean once a week and to be equally responsible for making sure the dustbin is put out on the right day. Also agree on what food is communal and what is not. Tea and coffee, sugar and bread are things everyone consumes, and you'll both be using the washing-up liquid and household cleaners. A good idea is to have a kitty to which you both contribute a fiver each week. Out of that kitty the very basic expenses of the household can be met.

Make sure the rent is paid regularly without your lodger having to be reminded about it every week or every month. This can be embarrassing and can cause a rift between you. The simplest answer is for the lodger to pay you by standing order. This way neither of you actually has to discuss the matter once the sum has been initially fixed.

Deciding how much rent to charge is going to depend on:

- the part of the country you're living in and the availability of rented accommodation in the area. A quick look through the property columns in the local paper will give some indication of the going rate for your neighbourhood;

- the position of the property in relation to shops and public transport, and whether there is a parking space available;

- the facilities on offer in your home, in particular the room you're renting out. Is it spacious enough to take the usual bedroom furniture and an extra armchair or small writing table? How well decorated is your home and is it reasonably well furnished?

Having worked out a figure, the next question is whether to

include the lodger's share of the heating and lighting bills in the rent. If you decide to combine the two, take into account the seasonal variations that occur in bills. Don't simply work out a contribution based on summer usage, when consumption is generally lower. A simpler method is to split the quarterly bills down the middle when heating, electricity and hot water seem to be used in equal amounts. If the television is on hire, why not halve the rental charge and the cost of the TV licence? But expect to hand over a refund if the lodger moves out before the year is over.

One expense which might not be so easy to divide down the middle is the telephone bill. Deciding to share the bill equally, before you know how many calls the new lodger will make and to where, means you run the risk of subsidising someone else's telephone conversations if they are the more prolific user. Logging each call made is tedious but can help divide the bill up fairly.

Finding the right person

As already stated, the best kind of lodger is probably someone already known to you. Be wary, however, about sharing with a colleague you work closely with. If you are with that person all day and come home to them each night as well, you will rapidly run out of things to talk about and may find you can never completely switch off from work.

If you decide to advertise for a lodger, be absolutely certain about whom you invite to move in. The main ways to find someone to share are to place a small ad in your local paper, put a card in the newsagent's window or a notice on the board of a local club.

Be specific about how you word the advertisement; the charge in a local newspaper will be based on the number of words. Don't let that put you off, however, from making it clear exactly the kind of lodger you are looking for. State whether you want to share with a man or a woman, what age range they should come within, and describe the facilities in your home. For instance, it's important to make it clear if they will be sharing all facilities and can only count on a bedroom as their own. Decide whether you want a non-smoker or not. Don't put your address in any advertisement, but use instead your home or work telephone number. Then sit back and wait for the rush!

Many people find interviewing a prospective lodger an embarrassing and uncomfortable experience. To find the right person, however, you must be prepared to ask the right questions. Your first indication of what the person is like will come when they telephone you in response to the advertisement. You can take the opportunity to ask a few basic questions and if you are then satisfied, invite them to have a look at the house or flat. When they come round, get chatting about the kind of life they lead and tell them about yours. Look for areas where friction might arise. After all, you may not like them to come home in the early hours with a different companion every night!

Explain what you are looking for in a lodger. If you want someone who will treat your house or flat as a home and not a hotel then say so. Make it clear which bills are shared and which household chores are done in turn. Find out about their job and whether the hours they'll be keeping are compatible with your own. Ask about their interests and what they do with their free time. Someone who's going to sit in front of the television each and every night might become rather tiresome.

Try and make the 'interview' a two-way exchange. Tell the person about yourself, your lifestyle, and what you expect from someone who is going to share at least part of it.

If all seems well, perhaps you could suggest going out for a drink to discuss the finer points of living together. Above all, don't rush into anything. Sharing with someone isn't easy, especially when you start out as total strangers. Communication and consideration on both sides are the two essential ingredients in learning to live with someone else. The situation is bound to feel awkward and strange at first as you each try to find out about the other without stepping on any toes.

If you are not sure that you will be able to live happily with any of the people who have contacted you, don't be afraid to admit that perhaps sharing your home is not a good idea after all. There is too much at stake to spoil your new-found freedom and independence for the sake of a bit of extra money each week.

Pets

There is one type of lodger for which permission isn't required from the bank or building society. It won't keep you awake with loud music, leave washing up in the sink and dirty clothes around the house. In short, it's a pet. But although a pet as a lodger has many advantages, there is one serious disadvantage – it doesn't pay any rent.

Nevertheless, a lot of people find that a pet provides the companionship they need without the inconvenience of having another person around the house. Pets, however, are not just for decoration. They do need care and attention, and feeding bills can be expensive. Should they ever require treatment from a vet, the cost begins to soar.

For someone living on their own and working full-time, the choice of pet is rather limited. It is very unfair on a dog that needs regular exercise to be cooped up inside all day. Cats are another matter entirely. Naturally independent, they are not too bothered if their owners disappear for the best part of the day. In fact they would hardly notice it, since their main role in life is to curl up and go to sleep.

Cats need very little looking after, particularly if you put in a cat flap which enables them to come and go as they please. A bowl of food a day, some water and a place to sleep are almost all they want. When you come home in the evening they'll look for a show of affection, and then spend the rest of the time in front of the fire. No wonder so many homes have cats.

The only possible drawback about providing a cat flap in the back door is that your moggie might be tempted to invite his or her friends in for a meal. Tom cats that have not been neutered have an unpleasant habit of spraying an area, indoors and out, to mark their territory. The smell is quite appalling and can linger for weeks. Since there are so many unwanted cats about looking for homes, it is wise to have your tom neutered and your female speyed, or you could soon find your home overrun with feline friends.

A little love goes a long way with cats, and they will rapidly become loyal and affectionate lodgers. They only object if you regularly go away for days at a time. A weekend is fine – you can leave enough food for them to get by – but if you intend to take regular breaks away, cats are not a good idea.

There is really very little choice over other kinds of pets. Guinea pigs and rabbits are suitable for someone away from home for the best part of a day, but they aren't exactly demonstrative. Neither are gerbils and hamsters, which can look after themselves provided their cages are regularly cleaned out. Cage birds can get lonely, particularly parrots which mope if left alone too long. The other practical choice of pet is fish, either the tropical variety which need an aquarium with all that goes with it, or the common or garden goldfish.

Keeping pets is a responsibility: they must be looked after properly, baskets or cages cleaned regularly, food provided, love reciprocated. Only get a pet if you are prepared to look after it properly, and that means meeting its needs and not abandoning it when you discover that there is more to its little life than a bowl of food.

COUPLES

Living with a lodger has its advantages and disadvantages, but at least you start from the basis that there is no personal commitment involved. You can even dislike each other but still live under the same roof, albeit with some difficulty. The bottom line is that you both have part of the house or flat to call your own and can retire there when the other person is getting on your nerves.

However, if you are planning to live together as a couple, you must be able to get on, at least for 99 per cent of the time. Learning to live together involves understanding one another's emotional and practical needs. The long-term success of a relationship often depends on the foundations laid at the beginning of the partnership.

A couple's expectations at this early stage are naturally riding high, especially when they move into their home as newlyweds. The wedding was probably the culmination of months of planning and preparation. The traditional ingredients of the bride in white, guests in all their finery and the ceremony itself will have put the couple on an emotional 'high'. Then of course there is a week or two of getting away from it all on honeymoon, perhaps spending the days lying in the sun beside a pool. All this must come close to most people's idea of a perfect wedding, and so it is not surprising that the weeks that follow can seem a bit of an anti-climax. Many couples experience post-wedding blues before settling down to their new life together.

It is a fact that while most couples spend months or even years planning and saving for a wedding, working out the tiniest details in advance, they give very little thought to what happens afterwards.

They don't discuss how they will actually live together, what sort of changes they can expect and how they will have to adapt to cope with them. Many people go into marriage with preconceived ideas of how it will work out afterwards and assume that everything will be fine. To reiterate the point once again, you never really know someone until you live with them, and when you actually start living together there may be a whole new side of your partner waiting to be discovered.

If you are the wife, has the man in your life grown accustomed to having a meal ready and waiting for him when he comes home from work? Has his mother always tidied up after him, and washed and ironed his clothes? If she has, there is the danger that he will expect the same from you. In short, you will take over where his doting mother left off. On the other hand, if you are the husband what kind of lifestyle did the woman in your life enjoy with her parents? Was she spoilt and never expected to lift a finger around the house? If so, she may find the commitment of marriage a nasty shock to begin with. Perhaps without really realising it, you may both be trying to create a carbon copy of your own parents' marriages. But what has worked for them (if indeed it has actually worked) may not be suitable for you.

Ideally, all this should have been discussed long ago. But if it hasn't and living together is providing a series of unpleasant surprises about what is expected of you, then the time to put things right is now. The pattern which starts to develop is likely to become the blueprint for the rest of your lives, so it is best to sort things out straightaway. If you don't like the role you are expected to play, say so. Discuss it, work it out, describe your feelings and try to understand your partner's point of view. Be prepared to change your ways or compromise on the issues you cannot agree on. Intransigence does not denote a strong character but an inflexible mind.

A flexible approach is often called for when working out who does what around the home. Ideally, you'll share all the chores. The idea that the wife does all the cooking, cleaning and washing while the husband occasionally puts up a shelf is a very old-fashioned one indeed. In households where both partners are working, there is no excuse whatsoever for not sharing duties equally.

If just the husband works, then he can be expected to lend a hand at the weekends. Contrary to popular opinion, some men actually welcome the opportunity to cook, though few would admit to a passion for cleaning. Cooking in particular is something which lends itself to being done together, and is the more enjoyable for it. After being brought up on what your parents like in the way of food, it's an opportunity to discover new tastes and dishes which you might otherwise have never considered. Try being a bit adventurous, if only to relieve the monotony of cooking the same thing on the same day each week. If you have a garden, why not have a barbecue occasionally?

Insurance companies occasionally publish the 'worth' of a woman at home all day while the man is out at work. The total he would otherwise have to pay to have his washing done, his house cleaned, his meals cooked, not to mention his children looked after, is staggering. It goes to show that a wife does actually work very hard even when she is not a wage-earner. Men who live in the dark ages and consider that a wife is an unpaid skivvy are not only fooling themselves but are also insulting their partners.

Sharing the load

If you both recognise that times have changed and men are now expected to play their part around the house, there should be no problem. If either of you came into marriage with the old ideas about who does what, and this isn't something that suits you both, a little re-education is required. It is important to get such problems out in the open, to discuss them and be prepared to shift your ground a little for the sake of a happy home life. But some people just can't see that they are not pulling their weight. The simplest answer is to stand your ground and refuse to do anything more than what you regard as your fair share. If you prepare the meals, make your partner do the washing up. If he or she won't, then don't cook another meal. It's drastic, but sometimes such a method is the only way to ram home the message: 'I am not here to wait on you!' If neither of you enjoys cooking, perhaps the answer is to invest in as many labour-saving devices as you can afford. Finding house room for a freezer and a microwave is a good start.

Your social life

Living together and having a social life will largely depend on how much cash is available. Paying a mortgage and meeting your bills will devour a sizeable chunk of your income. There is also the question of how much time you want to spend with each other outside the home.

Some couples believe that if you live together, you always go out together as a twosome. Other couples will sometimes want to go their own way. Trying to agree how often each partner goes out separately is one area in a relationship which is guaranteed to cause a row or two at some time. Once again, compromise may be called for. Couples who spend all their free time apart from each other are bound to feel the strain sooner or later; but there is nothing wrong with going out with your friends the odd night a week and leaving your other half to fend for him– or herself. The time to start worrying is when you prefer to go out with friends rather than with your partner.

If money is short, concentrate on entertaining at home. Invite friends for a drink, forgoing the idea of a full-blown meal. They are likely to bring a bottle with them, which cuts down the cost even more!

Living together for the first time calls for a great deal of understanding from both of you. Before, you may each have had active lives among a wide circle of friends, not necessarily the same circle. It is important, if you are to develop a strong relationship, to share each other's friends. Don't regard your partner's friends as a part of the past you would sooner forget. Make them welcome, but at the same time make sure they recognise that things have changed. You are the most important person in your partner's life now, and they shouldn't forget that.

It is also important that you both spend some time together outside the home, and going out with friends is not the complete answer. There are many other ways to enjoy yourselves, the cinema or theatre being the most obvious examples.

When things go wrong

It is extremely rare, but just occasionally you'll meet a couple who claim they never argue. It's possible they are telling the the truth, as they see it. But it is more likely that they have drifted so far apart that they might as well be living on different planets. They don't argue for the simple reason that they haven't really talked to each other for years.

In the real world, rows occur in any relationship between two people who have different opinions and are not afraid of expressing them.

On a rage rating of 1 to 10, how does your temper shape up? The hair-trigger reaction definitely deserves a high mark. Everything seems fine one minute, sparks are flying the next. Someone who is slow to anger may appear calm on the outside but inwardly the temperature is rising. If the pressure doesn't ease off, he or she erupts like a volcano.

How you deal with your partner's angry moods will depend on your own temperament. Two hair-trigger tempers will find control virtually impossible. They'll be in the middle of a row before they realise it, and probably secretly enjoying the high drama. Arguments will be rare when both sides are 'volcanic' types. They'll each know the telltale signs and retreat, afraid of the consequences. When there's an attraction of opposites, there may still be frequent rows but probably all one-sided. The more patient partner can either grow a thick skin or walk away until the more excitable partner has calmed down.

When a relationship is basically happy and sound, having a row merely clears the air and releases a lot of pent-up frustrations. But when two people are miserable with each other, the arguments are rarely therapeutic. Instead of an exchange of opinions, there are accusations and countercharges. Words are used to humiliate, and occasionally the verbal assault can give way to physical abuse.

The cause is seldom straightforward, and in some cases the attacker is repeating history. As a child he or she may have witnessed parents hitting one another. Almost invariably it is the woman who is battered, and such an assault can end the relationship. Promises that it won't happen again are easy to make and easy to break. Seeking professional help, to understand why it happened, may be the first step to controlling such aggression, and should be the victim's main condition for staying.

There are organisations on hand which can help when a relationship begins to break down through a partner's unreasonable behaviour, such as violent attacks, excess drinking or perhaps a sexual problem.

The local GP may be able to provide direct help, or can refer the couple to marriage guidance, which is open to both married and unmarried couples. Counsellors are trained to help couples find their own solution. The answers have to come from the two people involved and not from concerned relatives, however good their intentions.

There is often only a fine line between being offered advice from the family and being confronted with blatant interference. We've all heard the in-law jokes, but when it's happening to you it doesn't seem as funny. Some parents have difficulty accepting that the original family relationship is no longer the primary one in their child's life. Distance may preclude all parental interference, but if the family live in the same area and you feel they are becoming too actively involved, the remedy lies in polite but persistent refusal.

The softly, softly approach is likely to ruffle fewer feathers than an out-and-out row. It's not compulsory that you should like your partner's parents, but be careful about letting it show. Your partner's first loyalty is to you, the person he or she has chosen to spend the rest of his or her life with, but that doesn't mean he or she wants to sever all ties with their family. Even when there has been opposition to the development of a relationship, a marriage or taking the decision to live together can be a new beginning. Even superficial politeness is better than open warfare, and there may come a day when you need their support.

The important thing when you feel unhappy with your partner is to accept the fact and face the problem. Only then can you start doing something about it. The last thing you should do is pretend the difficulties don't exist or simply hope they will go away.

The first stage in solving a problem is to talk about it to your partner. Only through frank discussion can you begin to come to terms with what is wrong. It may well be that by doing this you can solve the problem yourselves and not have to go to someone outside the relationship. Be totally honest with each other: it may be that one of you is simply not aware of how the other one feels. Above all, don't panic. Most problems can be solved given time, patience and understanding.

5
Furnishing your home and counting the cost

FURNITURE

As a first-time buyer, you probably haven't had the opportunity to buy and store much furniture. The likelihood is that you have been living with your family or renting furnished accommodation. This chapter assumes that you are starting from scratch and at the same time trying to furnish your home as cheaply as possible.

If you are operating on a shoestring, accept from the beginning that a little has got to go a long way. Don't even start dreaming of luxuries until the basics have been worked out. If you have brought a fairly large property, concentrate on finding furniture for the rooms which are going to be in immediate use. To make your money go further, you may have to buy quite a few items second-hand. Before deciding on where to start looking, however, work out the bare minimum you are going to need. Begin with the three main rooms: sitting-room, kitchen and bedroom.

- *Sofa or two armchairs*. Having at least something to sit on seems fairly essential. But if you feel comfort can take a back seat in your furnishing plans, then floor cushions would be a cheaper alternative.
- *Television set*. This could be considered a very important item, especially if you're living on your own. Calculate whether buying a TV outright is going to dig too deeply into your savings or whether hire purchase would be more feasible, although it will cost extra in the long run. The third option is to hire the telly from a rental firm.

Furnishing your home and counting the cost · **53**

This way the repairs are often carried out free of charge, but on the other hand you could end up paying for the set several times over.

- *Dining-table and four chairs.* These are nice to have for proper sit-down meals and when staging dinner parties for friends. If happiness is eating with a tray on your knee, however, and you're not planning to entertain in a formal way, perhaps a coffee table will suffice.

- *Cooker.* One of the most vital pieces of equipment in the home. It's not so much a decision of whether to have one or not but rather what type, gas or electric. The fixtures left by the previous owners and what you have cooked on in the past will have some bearing on your decision. However, both the gas and electricity boards maintain that converting over needn't be that expensive if the main supply is easily accessible. With some new cookers the conversion is thrown in free of charge.

  Advocates of gas point out that running costs are cheaper, there's instant heat control (ideal for when the milk is about to boil over) and a gas cooker is as clean as an electric one. 'Oh no, it's not,' say devotees of electricity, who insist their way of cooking is cleaner. They also claim that siting an electric cooker in a kitchen is easier, there's the added attraction of ceramic hobs, and now the new halogen cookers provide almost instant heat control. The halogen light power elements can achieve full power in seconds and go to zero at the touch of a button, but such technology doesn't come cheap.

- *Fridge.* It is certainly possible to live without a fridge although not always convenient. Trying to keep butter, milk and meat fresh in summer is going to be a headache, and a cooler box isn't really the answer for daily use. But if you are moving into your new home in winter and it hasn't got central heating to warm up the kitchen, having no fridge shouldn't be such a hardship.

- *Washing machine and tumble-drier.* It's nice to have both, but the closeness and the facilities of the local launderette may sway your decision. If the launderette is only a short distance away, you may decide to take all your clothes there, or else just buy a spin-drier and wash small items at home.
- *Cupboards.* It's rare but not unknown for the previous owners to take all or some of the kitchen cupboards with them. If there's insufficient storage space on the walls, consider either buying self-assembly units or putting up open shelves. The only drawback to the latter is that exposed surfaces in kitchens get very sticky.
- *Vegetable and pan racks.* Cheap and cheerful, and they don't take up much room. The deep wells of the vegetable rack can also be used to store other miscellaneous items such as oven gloves and tea towels.
- *Bed.* Possibly the most important item of furniture. Try to buy a sound mattress even when money is tight; otherwise, you might pay for it with a bad back and sleepless nights.
- *Drawers and wardrobes.* There is plenty of choice in the second-hand market, but a cheaper alternative is to turn a bedroom alcove into a wardrobe. All you need is a piece of dowelling fastened across the space and, if there's room, shelves on either side for jumpers, etc. Hide it all from view with curtains or a large blind.
- *Curtains.* Frosted glass in the loo and bathroom might reduce the need for curtains or blinds, but you will require something to protect privacy in the living-room and bedroom. If someone in your family or a friend donates a pair of curtains which turn out to be too short, don't discard them. They can be made to fit by sewing similar-textured material along the bottom and down one or two sides of each curtain. As long as you don't

put a lightweight cloth on a heavyweight, or vice versa, the curtains' folds should still hang reasonably well.

- *Carpets*. On a practical level these do cut down on draughts through the floorboards and make a room feel and look cosier. The appearance of second-hand carpets can be substantially improved by cleaning with a recommended shampoo.

Once the bare minimum in furniture and furnishings has been worked out, the next stage is to consider where to start looking. The first place must surely be within your own immediate circle. Ask around to see if anyone has any odd pieces of furniture they want to unload. A kindly relative might come up with a chest of drawers or an old pair of curtains. When the prospect of sitting on wooden boxes begins to loom large, be grateful for anything. Remember that it's not so much what it looks like now, but what it could look like after it's been stripped and repainted or has a new covering. The relative or friend may even store it for you until you are ready to pick it up.

Second-hand: Sorting out the treasure from the trash

Acquiring a few bits and bobs from family and friends means your savings are going to stretch that much further. Deciding to buy all or some of your furniture and electrical goods from second-hand dealers will also increase your spending power – but there are risks. No one's going to point out the faults; you are going to have to spot them yourself.

It doesn't require expert training to detect problems or weaknesses in an old piece of furniture. A careful inspection should reveal any drawbacks, and one of the most common faults is woodworm. The telltale signs are tiny holes in the wood's surface. This condition can be treated, but if the pests aren't killed they can spread throughout your home. Never leave furniture which is infested with woodworm standing on bare boards: that's asking for trouble.

Remember also to open and close drawers to make sure they 'run' easily. If they don't, try and negotiate a discount. In some cases the remedy is to rub the runners with candlewax. Check on the condition of the door hinges on cabinets and wardrobes. Loose screws can be replaced, but repairing split wood around a hinge is a far trickier operation. Buying second-hand gives you the opportunity to bring about a transformation and make an item unique. Although some pieces may be dirty now, try and see the furniture's potential.

However, when you buy second-hand electrical equipment, your criteria are different. You are looking for reliability, but how do you spot that? It's certainly no use going on appearances alone. Just because a washing machine has been regularly cleaned on the outside, there is no guarantee that the motor isn't faulty. Whenever possible, ask for a demonstration. It won't take long to prove that a fridge or an iron is working. There's no reason why a few clothes can't be put inside a spin-drier to see how the drum copes with weight. But it's not going to be feasible to set a washing machine going in a shop. That's why it is advisable to look for retailers operating a parts' warranty scheme. Your local trading standards department may be able to recommend a reputable dealer selling second-hand electrical equipment, or at the very least pinpoint the shops which have recently been prosecuted following consumer complaints.

The law does offer some protection whether you are buying new or second-hand goods. The Sale of Goods Act stipulates that everything you buy from a retailer should be in full working order unless faults are pointed out to you during the sale. However, when you are intending to buy second-hand, consider the age of the item, how much you are paying for it, and how long you can reasonably expect it to last. These three factors will have some bearing on the validity of your claim if you should need to make one.

Searching the 'nearly new' shops is one way to furnish

your home, but you may prefer to buy privately through the 'For Sale' columns in local papers. At least you will see the item in its home environment and be able to find out why it's being sold (as long as you feel the owners are telling the truth). Your legal rights in private sales are limited. Your only comeback is if the item varies from its description in the advert, so check the wording carefully and, again, ask for a demonstration wherever possible.

Another popular option when buying second-hand is the auction sale. Consumer rights are restricted, as the rules are made by the auctioneer. The circumstances and surroundings of the auction will dictate whether you will have the chance to check everything over thoroughly. However, you are more likely to buy an item at a cheaper price in an auction than in a 'nearly new' shop.

Second-hand dealers accumulate their stock of furniture through house clearances and visiting auction sales. If you have the time and the transport to collect the items, why not cut out the middleman and buy direct from the auction? When general household goods are going under the hammer, the sale is normally advertised in the local press and on general noticeboards in the area. Auctioneers either have their own premises or hire local halls. If you haven't seen any furniture sales advertised, ring up a few auctioneers listed in the Yellow Pages and ask for a catalogue for their next sale of domestic goods.

The usual practice is that items going in a formal auction are given a lot number. They are introduced by that figure to eliminate any confusion. Even when it is too big to lift up and show off to the assembled throng, everyone knows exactly what is being bid for. The auctioneers normally arrange a viewing time before the sale begins to allow the public to have a good look around. There may be stewards on hand to move any items so would-be buyers can get an overall view.

After making your selection, mark in your catalogue the price you are willing to pay for each item. Regard these figures as your limit and stick to them. Should you get carried away in the excitement of bidding, you'll leave having spent far more than originally intended. Visiting an auction saleroom for the first time can be a bit of a shock, if you imagined they resembled the scenes on TV where an art treasure is secured by a nod and a wink. When there's standing room only and people are moving about, you may have to wave your arm and shout out your bid rather than simply winking at the man with the hammer.

Even if you haven't been selective and have had to buy the cheapest items, or fill up your home with furniture from other people, it is still possible to create a theme or at least a feeling of continuity amid the assortment of styles. The answer lies in distracting the eye away from the actual outline and into the main body of the piece. One way to achieve this is by decorating the furniture with a design. If you think that might be stretching your artistic talents too far, there are plenty of aids on the market to help you. It doesn't take much skill to hold a stencil and dab or spray the paint through the pattern's holes.

If you want a less stylised approach, the marbled look is easy to reproduce. Paint the furniture in one colour and use a strong feather to trace on a slightly darker shade for that mottled appearance. Alternatively, items of furniture can be camouflaged by painting them the same colour as their background. An ugly sideboard can be made to merge into its setting by using this method.

The selected use of one colour to bring out special features can effectively build up a theme, or you can paint all the furniture in the same colour to create the illusion of a set. Several contrasting colours in one room, for instance a purple patterned carpet and an orange sofa, can seem less out of tune if they are brought together in some way. Perhaps harmony could be achieved if you found a length of material combining similar colours which could be made into a pair of curtains, cushion covers or even a tablecloth left permanently draped. The colourful union can then become the focal point of the room.

Eye-catching features can be further highlighted with

an angled lamp or spotlights. (An ideal opportunity to experiment with lights is if your new home needs rewiring. As you're working out where to site the sockets, consider whether to introduce spotlights on the ceiling or walls.) Otherwise, the light itself can become a focal point if the lampshade is big enough or strikingly decorated. Some of the materials used in the manufacture of lampshades are highly inflammable and may carry a warning not to use any light bulbs over a certain wattage. If in doubt, ask the advice of a trained assistant as to which bulb is best suited to your lighting needs. Forty watts is considered low, 60 watts is medium, and high power starts from around 150 watts. The common-strength light bulb used for living-rooms is 100 watts. A 60-watt bulb is advisable for reading lamps.

The do-it-yourself approach

Bargain hunters may also consider buying self-assembly furniture. In the big stores there's usually a demonstration model made up of each line being sold. This time, instead of looking for signs of wear and tear, you are going to try and assess how the furniture will stand up to daily use.

Are the hinges sturdy? What are the panels made of? Does it look as if the doors will fit snugly? Most items are put together with the aid of a mallet and screwdriver, but if you are unsure ask a store assistant whether any additional tools are required. Before attempting to assemble the pieces, check that every item has been included. Have a few dry runs, loosely putting the pieces together before applying any force or any glue.

One piece of furniture which is sometimes difficult to assemble correctly is the dining-table chair. If the legs aren't fitted properly, the chair is going to have a permanent wobble. If this does happen, either sand down the legs until they are all equal or, if there is too much discrepancy, the alternative is to add extra length to the shorter legs. What's needed for this is a small section of dowelling. Ideally, it shouldn't be more than half the leg's circumference. Trim the dowelling and stick it to the bottom of the chair leg. The repair should be strong enough to take the weight and be so small that it is unobtrusive.

Making the most of space

So far we have concentrated on ways to minimise the cost of setting up home by buying second-hand or self-assembly furniture. A different approach may be called for, however, if you're still working to a tight budget but there isn't much space available.

Many flat dwellers find the answer is to opt for modern dual-purpose or fold-away furniture when the criterion is maximum amount of use for minimum space. New designs are coming out all the time, so shop around to get an overall view of what's on offer before buying anything. In recent years dual-purpose sofas and chairs have been on the best-sellers list. Sit on them by day and sleep on them at night. Constant use may eventually affect the sofa or chair's ability to retain an exact sitting position. A holding strap or catch on the side will help reinforce the vertical hold.

Keep bedroom furniture to a minimum by investing in a combined desk and bed unit. Study and store items go underneath and you sleep on top, or there's always the more traditional bed with drawers in the base.

To make the most of available space in your home, you may have to break with convention. The traditional place for the washing machine, spinner and drier has been the kitchen. But what happens when the kitchen is too small to take them? You will have to find an alternative. Is the hallway large enough, or is there room upstairs if the cost of new plumbing isn't prohibitive? Initially, there will be extra work involved during installation, but there's no other reason why the kitchen's monopoly can't be broken.

Avoid cluttering up floor space by thinking of ways to use spare ceiling and wall space. When drying clothes is likely

Furnishing your home and counting the cost · 61

to be a problem, rig up a drying rack and pulley over the bath. Much better than filling up the living-room or bedroom with a clothes horse. In the kitchen, why not keep vegetables in a line of chain baskets suspended from the ceiling, rather than taking up valuable floor space with a traditional rack? Is there room to fit wire storage baskets on to the backs of cabinet doors? Could a few shelves be put higher up the wall and stacked with items which are seldom used? With a little ingenuity you may suddenly discover valuable storage areas which are often overlooked.

FINANCE

A crucial aspect of home ownership is learning how to handle your financial affairs. All of a sudden the first-time buyer has to start thinking about mortgage payments, the community charge (poll tax), rates and fuel bills, and when to pay them. It might sound daunting, but it needn't be if you take the time to draw up a detailed picture of all your outgoings. One way of balancing the books is to commit yourself to a 12-month spending plan.

Budget accounts

One of the easiest methods of doing this is to open a special budget account at your bank. You'll be required to list all your major bills and expenses for the coming year. The sum total is then divided by 12 and this final figure will be the amount transferred each month from your account to your new budget account. The bank will issue you with a special cheque book for this account. This way you can keep a track of your spending, and the bank will not be unduly worried if you slip into the red some months where you have particularly high bills. They will know that over the course of the year, things should balance out.

Attempting to forecast every bill which is going to arrive

over the next 12 months is difficult. To jog your memory, begin by dividing your anticipated spending into four categories: home, travel, leisure and personal.

- *Home.* First on the list are your mortgage repayments and your rates bill or community charge. Mortgage payments can fluctuate with the rise and fall in interest rates, so don't assume that what you need to pay at the start of the year will be the same at the end of it. The community charge is being phased in and will operate throughout the country by April 1990. In the past, rates have depended on the rateable value of your property, but the personal community charge (or poll tax) is a flat-rate tax payable by all adults aged 18 or over (unless they qualify for special exemptions). The level of poll tax will be set yearly by the local authorities. It will be the same sum for every adult, irrespective of size of property or income.

  Electricity and gas bills are sent out quarterly. If you didn't ask the previous owners for a guide to the cost of lighting and heating, see if any relatives or friends can give you an idea of how expensive their heating system is in relation to the way they use it. If your home is heated by coal or oil, don't forget to add the price of fuel to your plan and add on extra to cover inflation.

  Telephone bills also arrive every three months. The television licence is an annual payment, and if you rent a set you will have to pay either monthly or weekly. This section can also cover house and contents insurance, as well as any hire purchase agreement or loan repayments of any kind.

- *Travel.* If you run a car or motorbike, consider the actual cost of filling it up with petrol, as well as buying a tax disc and getting it through its annual MOT. Also allow an amount each month to cover the cost of repairs. If you travel by public transport, add up the cost of your train, tube or bus ticket, and allow for the inevitable rises.

- *Leisure.* This category includes any holiday or visit you are planning in the next 12 months, as well as subscriptions to clubs and magazines.

- *Personal.* Estimate your weekly food bill, and how much you expect to spend on clothes and presents for birthdays and Christmas.

You should now have some idea of your major outgoings for the year and an indication of how much you'll have to pay into your budget account each month in order to meet them. The drawback with a budget account is that the bank may well levy a service charge. To avoid this expense, you may decide to operate your own long-term financial plan.

Going it alone

The essence of successful budgeting lies in the planning: you know when the bills are due and how you're going to pay them. To maintain an overall view, list your financial commitments on a 12-month wall planner. Include all your regular bills and mark down when you expect them. This at-a-glance guide is invaluable in keeping a check on your spending. The next step is to estimate how much money you're going to need each month for food, clothes and your social life.

Now at least you know what your outgoings are. At this point your worst fears may be confirmed as the realisation sinks in that there are going to be some months when the pay cheque won't stretch far enough. Go back to your original calculations and see if it's possible to save some money during the months when you expect fewer or lower bills. If it still looks as though it is going to be difficult to raise the necessary cash for a particularly high bill, consider spreading the cost with monthly payments.

Easy payment terms

Many organisations which send out regular bills have come to the conclusion that they are far more likely to get their money if they make it easier for their customers to pay, so they have developed a variety of easy payment schemes. Most local councils allow you to pay your community charge or rates in twelve equal instalments, either by a standing order from your bank account or with a special payments book.

Gas and electricity boards have a scheme in which they estimate your consumption for a year and ask you to make regular monthly or weekly payments. The theory is that you will pay slightly more than you would otherwise during the summer and slightly less during the winter. At the end of the year they'll advise you of the difference and either ask you to settle up or reimburse you, whichever is the case. You'll receive quarterly statements as opposed to bills, so you'll always know whether you are in credit or lagging behind. However, if you fail to keep your side of the bargain in making the regular payments, you will lose the benefit of paying in this way.

To avoid being faced with having to pay your telephone bill or television licence in one fell swoop, consider buying special stamps each week or month which are then deducted from your bill. British Telecom has also introduced a payments scheme similar to those used by the gas and electricity boards.

Money-saving ideas

Joining easy payment schemes is one immediate way of making your wages go further, but at the end of the day you are still going to be paying out the same sum of money. While you are trying to organise your financial affairs, why not see if you can begin to reduce some of your expenses by introducing a few changes in your style of living?

Does home ownership mean that, initially, you're going to

have to tighten your belt? Have you allowed too much for going out with friends? Are there cheaper ways to socialise? Can the figures set aside for housekeeping be whittled down a little bit further? No one's suggesting a diet of boiled rice, but a change in eating habits may add to the change in your purse. The cash-conscious shopper goes for the cheaper cuts of meat instead of prime cuts, and buys supermarket own brands rather than well-known names.

Eating less expensive meals is one obvious way to reduce food bills, but what about heating costs? There are ways to cut down on your heating bills that won't cost you a penny. Could you tolerate turning down the central heating thermostat or heater controls? A reduction of 1 °C has been shown to cut heating costs by as much as 10 per cent. Throughout the year that can add up to quite a substantial saving. It doesn't cost anything to put on another jumper, and during the night pile on extra blankets rather than leave the heating on, unless there is a real risk of burst pipes. Be more economical with the central heating timer. Rather than setting the system to come on an hour before getting up, set the clock for only 15 minutes ahead.

Are you needlessly wasting money while you are cooking? Instead of using two or three pans for vegetables, is it sometimes possible to cook them in just one pan, or to use a pan with segmented sections? Keep lids on pans and remember to reduce heat once the contents have boiled. Pressure cookers save on gas and electricity when they are used to cook complete dishes.

Try planning your main meals so that each time you cook, the oven is used to full capacity. Resist the temptation to keep opening the oven door while the food is cooking. If you have any small cooking appliances, get into the habit of using them: a slow cooking pot, a contact grill and a microwave oven all use less electricity than a big cooker. Remember to wash your pots in a bowl and never clean them under hot running water. Dripping taps waste more hot water than you think, so fix them. Instead of having a long soak in the bath, get into the habit of using a shower.

66 · *Setting up Home*

If you haven't got one then be more frugal with the bath water.

Keeping warm economically

Houses lose heat through their walls, windows, chimneys, doors, floors and lofts (Fig. 2). In the end all the heat has to escape somehow, but in an uninsulated house a large percentage escapes *before* you have had a chance to benefit

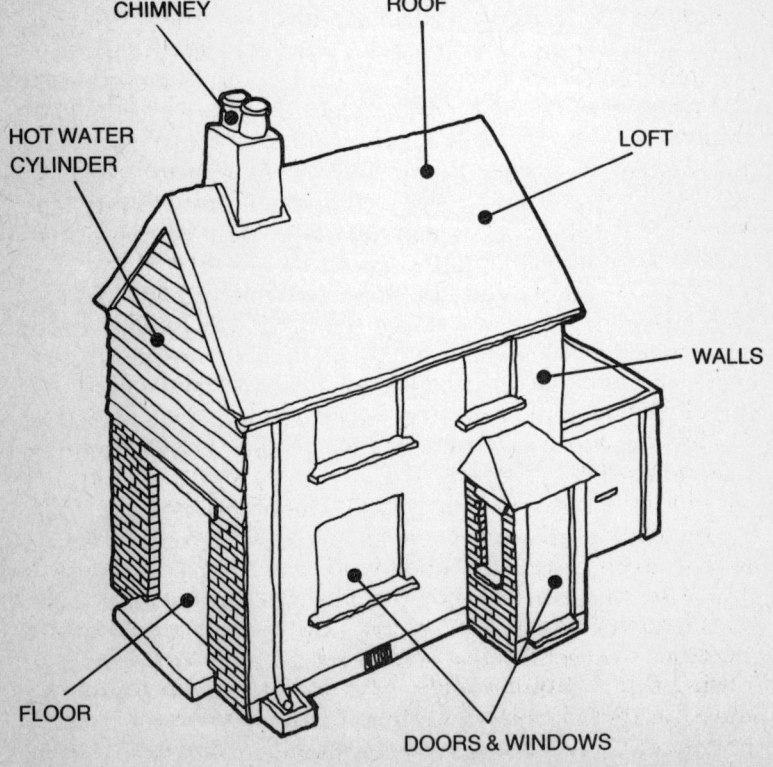

Fig 2

from it. The actual heat loss depends on the particular house. Homes with flat roofs lose more than traditional houses with pitched roofs. However, a little time and money spent now on insulation and draughtproofing will save money in the long run in any situation.

Insulating your home will involve some expense, but costs can be reduced by applying for a grant from the local authority. Cavity wall insulation is a job for the professionals, but no great DIY skills are called for to lag a hot water tank (recommended lagging jacket 80 mm [3 in]), insulate the loft and draughtproof external doors and windows with weatherproofing.

Lagging pipes or hot water tanks involves wrapping insulation material around them (fig. 3). The purpose of lagging the hot water system is to keep the *heat in*, thereby reducing your fuel bill. The purpose of lagging the cold water system is to keep the *cold out*, to stop pipes freezing and bursting. About a quarter of all heat lost goes through cracks and gaps around doors and windows, so draughtproofing, even if this simply means putting curtains on the windows and sand-filled tubes of fabric across the bottom of the door, makes economic sense. Contrary to popular opinion, not much heat is lost through the glass itself, so double glazing takes a long time to pay for itself.

The economists at British Gas have worked out that a couple living in a detached house could save £95 a year simply by adding loft insulation, weatherstripping and a cylinder jacket. It makes you stop and think, doesn't it? Would the savings be worth the initial outlay?

You may ask yourself the same question if you have electric storage heating and are thinking of switching to Economy 7. The term 'Economy 7' refers to the seven hours at night when the price of electricity is reduced to less than half the standard domestic rate. At the end of the seven hours, usually at 8 am during British Summertime, the tariff is put up to the day rate. But there is a sting in the tail. The Economy 7 daytime rate is sometimes higher than the standard domestic charge, which remains the same 24 hours a day.

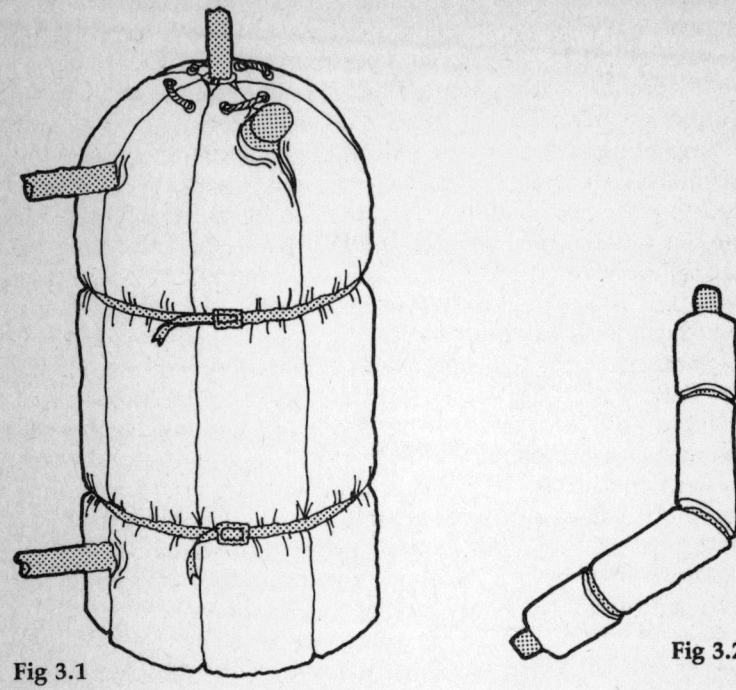

Fig 3.1

Fig 3.2

Finding ways of cutting your bills down to size may mean the difference between staying in the black and dipping into the red. But when you have a tight budget you need some kind of safety net for when the unexpected happens. If you have a credit card, keep it clear for these occasions, or think about a bank loan which would involve lower rates of interest. Your bank manager may be sympathetic to your change in circumstances, and might then be more tolerant of an account which has a tendency to show debit rather than credit.

Sharing the costs

As well as saving money by being more economical, you may decide an answer to your financial difficulties lies in sharing household expenses with someone else. Chapter four looked at ways of finding a lodger and assessing how compatible he or she would be with your own personality and lifestyle. It also dealt with the question of rent. But there is no point in scrimping and saving, taking a shower when you want a bath and putting on a jumper instead of turning up the fire, if your lodger is going to be extravagant. If he or she insists on making the rooms feel like ovens, then the rent should reflect this. And if the telephone is an essential part of the lodger's life, then you must make absolutely sure that he or she is paying a fair share of the bill.

Lodgers can be very expensive if the person concerned happens to be selfish and does not consider the bills he or she is happily running up. But the lodger might take the view that since he or she is paying an apparently high rent, then he or she is entitled to use the facilities of the house to his or her heart's content. It all comes down to fixing a fair rent, with neither of you exploiting the other.

Moonlighting

Since you have gone to such lengths to establish your independence and gain some privacy, you might not like the idea of a lodger intruding upon them. You could therefore always boost your income by taking a part-time job, by moonlighting. Busy pubs, for instance, thrive on part-time labour, and by taking a job serving behind the bar you will get the additional benefit of meeting new people.

There is a difference between casual labour and a proper part-time job. If you are employed on a casual basis, you may be paid cash-in-hand, and it is you who are obliged in law to tell the taxman. If you don't declare your extra earnings, the taxman may find out and will be after you to pay your dues. There can be few things worse than receiving a hefty tax demand when you thought you had successfully avoided the attentions of the Inland Revenue. Honesty is the best course.

If you take a formal part-time job while you are employed on a full-time basis somewhere else, your extra earnings will be liable to tax at the basic rate. Your new employer should tell the Inland Revenue that you are on the payroll and that they are making deductions from your wages. But it is again up to you to inform the Revenue as well. You can do this either through the office which deals with your main wages, or through the branch dealing with your part-time employer.

Consider carefully the pros and cons of taking on an extra job. It means a whole new set of commitments, and may drastically cut down the amount of time you have to yourself or for going out with friends. It could also leave you physically exhausted and unable to concentrate properly on your main job. But many people find part-time work an exciting change from their normal employment, and the extra money is always useful.

Dealing with crises

Having a thorough understanding of how far your money will stretch is one way to avoid some financial problems. But not everything can be spotted on the horizon, and every now and again you will be faced with a situation which calls for money, and a fair amount of it. It might be your car grinding to a permanent halt, some unpredicted expense or, worst of all, losing your job.

As has already been stated, the bank manager is the first port of call when a financial crisis threatens. Although he or she may not always show it, a bank manager does have an interest in your well-being. A temporary overdraft or short-term loan are two ways the manager can help you get things straightened out again. It is far better being honest with your bank manager and going to see him or her or a member of the staff than to carry on writing out cheques which may bounce. If the bank manager knows you are in difficulty, he or she will be far more ready to lend a helping hand and your cheques will continue to be honoured.

Far more serious, though, than a temporary crisis is losing your job. Once again, all the people who have a financial stake in your home must be told straightaway. The building society or bank may suspend your mortgage payments for a while, or simply require you to pay the interest on the loan without tackling the loan itself.

The Department of Health and Social Security offers assistance with mortgage interest to homeowners receiving Income Support, which is a Social Security benefit to help people who do not have enough money to live on. Income Support can be used to help pay the interest on mortgages or home loans. During the first 16 weeks, for people under 60, an amount will be added on to the Income Support payment to cover half the interest they have to pay. After 16 weeks, the claimant will receive a sum to cover all the interest.

Even if you have savings of £3,000 or less, it will not make any difference to a claim for Income Support. However, savings of between £3,000 and £6,000 will make a difference. The DHSS regards each £250 or part of £250 as if it were bringing in £1 a week. A partner's savings will also be counted.

Although there is help on hand, it is a sad fact that there are many homeowners who, faced with unemployment, stick their heads in the sand and hope the world will forget about them. It won't. To illustrate the point, let's look at what is likely to happen if you let the bills mount up.

Failure to pay the first half of a general rates bill will precipitate a further demand for the whole lot, and a warning that legal action will be taken if the money isn't forthcoming by the specified date. Miss a few instalments on the community charge and a similar procedure will follow.

The threatened legal action is likely to be an order to appear at court unless the outstanding sum, including legal costs incurred so far by the council, is paid. Even if you don't turn up, the magistrates have the power to proceed in your absence. They can order a bailiff to call and take away possessions.

The gas, water and electricity boards may cut off supplies

if their bills aren't paid and no compromise can be reached. To avoid such drastic measures, the Electricity Council and British Gas circulate advice leaflets to help domestic customers with financial worries. They urge consumers either to go directly to a showroom for advice, or to contact the local Electricity Consultative Council or the Gas Consumers' Council as well as the Citizens' Advice Bureau.

Debts can be either reduced through instalments or, if practical, by fitting a slot or card meter which would be adjusted to collect the debt within a set period. If the debt has only been incurred by buying a gas or electrical appliance through hire purchase, the supplies will not be cut off.

Having possessions confiscated and services disconnected sounds pretty grim, but such actions are standard practice if no compromise agreement can be reached between the two sides. The message which comes over loud and clear is, if you should lose your job, seek advice before the situation gets out of hand. There are people who can help.

A useful address in such situations is the Gas Consumers' Council, Abford House, 15 Wilton Road, Victoria, London SW1V 1LT for advice on your gas bill; for advice on your electricity bill look in the telephone directory for the number of your local Electricity Consultative Council.

6
Decorating and do-it-yourself guide

DECORATING

The secret of successful decorating lies in taking your time and not rushing the job. Allow yourself at least a month or two in your new home before attempting any painting or wallpapering projects. The delay will help you develop a better understanding of your new home. On a practical level, you'll be aware of how the light and shade change during the day. Perhaps a room may have a certain atmosphere which will suggest a particular design or style. Selecting colours on impulse, with no thought to the mood or effect they will create, is more likely to obscure a room's good points than to enhance them.

The immense variety of paints available nowadays means that there is literally something for everyone's palette. Each paint company has its own special branded lines which have been created for it and which will only be found under its label. But there is also a range of paints governed by the British Standards Institution which sets down a specific formula for each colour. Paint bearing the letters BS followed by a figure will be a uniform colour whichever company is marketing it.

The colour cards produced by the paint manufacturers give an up-to-date picture of what's available, and they sometimes offer advice in a special mix-and-match section. Deciding which colours to choose can be difficult, especially if you have never decorated before. A starting-point may be to think about your own responses to different colours. Yellows and reds are meant to be warm and friendly, greens are supposed to be relaxing, and blues suggest cleanness, even coolness. Do these primary colours provoke the same reactions from you? Study how your family and friends have used colours in their homes. Once you begin to analyse feelings in relation to colours, you become much more aware of the world around you.

Nowadays many more companies are beginning to understand the power of the paint brush as they experiment with the colour-conscious approach. It's probably no coincidence that a growing number of offices are painted in busy colours, while the canteen is a reflective green. How you plan to use the rooms in your own home may have some bearing on your final selection. A living room in one house could be a hive of industry, yet in another it's a place to relax and watch television, listen to music or read a book. Busy, warm colours would suit one, where quiet shades are better for another. The same approach can apply to the kitchen. If it's a busy, bustling room in the morning the decor might reflect this; however, if you like a nice peaceful start to the day, go for subtle tones.

Creating illusions

Colours can not only create moods but also produce optical illusions. White or light colours can be used to create a feeling of space. Low ceilings appear higher when painted with lighter shades. Alternatively, a deep colour will bring a high ceiling down, especially if the tops of the walls are also painted in the same tone. Rectangular rooms can be made to appear a little more square by drawing in the two smaller end walls with a darker colour than that used on the side walls. The same rule applies with a narrow corridor. Light colours on the long walls can make the passageway seem wider, and darker tones on the end walls will bring them in.

Introducing too many colours into one room, however, will lead to an almost continuous struggle for dominance. A better plan is to use one dominant colour to highlight special features such as ceiling cornices.

Wallpaper can also be used to great effect. Small prints make a room look spacious while large patterns seem to gobble up space. When selecting wallpaper, it is crucial to try and visualise the overall look so that you don't end up with a design that is going to clash with the curtains or sofa. Some paint shops allow customers to take wallpaper sample books home. They can then see at a glance if the paper they like goes with their furnishings.

Working out quantity and quality

Most wallpapers are the standard 520 mm ($20^{1}/_{2}$ in) wide and 10 m (11 yds) in length. When measuring up, add on a little extra for fitting. Allow 100 mm (about 4 in) for plain papers such as woodchip, but wastage may well be higher for a large pattern. If in doubt, ask a shop assistant to calculate the allowance figure for you.

The major manufacturers market their paints in standard size tins: 500 ml (0.88 pt), 1 l (1.76 pt), 2.5 l (0.55 gal) and 5 l (1.10 gal). The surface area the paint will cover is usually indicated on the side of the tin. The amount required will vary depending on the type and the condition of the surface you are planning to paint.

Despite the seemingly endless array of paints for household decorating, there are basically two types, oil and emulsion based. The gloss paints are oil based and have been specifically developed for use on wood and metal, including radiators. Alkyds or manmade resins such as polyurethane are also added to the paint to improve its durability and finish.

The ordinary gloss finish goes further than the non-drip variety. A rough estimate suggests that 1 l (1.76 pt) of ordinary paint covers between 15 and 17 sq m (18 to 20 sq yds), while non-drip gloss covers around 12 sq m (13 sq yds) per litre on a normal working surface. The ordinary gloss, however, has a very liquid consistency, and has a tendency to run if applied too thickly.

The oil-based paint group can also offer a silky eggshell finish as well as a gloss finish. Oil-based paints can be used on window frames, walls and metal. However, look carefully at suggestions on usage. Paints with a washable finish are particularly suited for rooms with a high moisture level such as the kitchen or bathroom.

Emulsion-based paints are water based and quick drying. They cover between 13 and 14 sq m (16 to 17 sq yds) per litre and are ideal for walls and ceilings. When emulsion is applied to a woodchip paper or one of the more heavy-duty relief papers, no undercoat is needed. But if you are planning to cover a bare plaster wall with emulsion, you will need to apply a sealant first. Watered-down emulsion usually does the job, although walls which are particularly porous may require a special primer sealer. If in doubt ask for advice at the nearest decorating centre, or ring up the information services run by many of the big paint manufacturers.

Preparations for decorating

Woodwork, walls and ceilings need to be properly cleaned and prepared before attempting to paint or hang wallpaper. How much work is going to be involved will depend on the condition of the timber and plaster. For woodwork, if the old paint is in a reasonable condition and the wood is sound, your preparations may involve just a gentle rub with glass paper in readiness for the new paint. But if the surface is uneven and flaking, a more vigorous attack may be called for.

Glass paper will still do the job, as long as you have plenty of time and sufficient muscle power. A more expedient method, however, is to use an ordinary scraper or one with a triangular metal face (the latter is ideal for getting into corners). Both tools can be used with a blow-torch. The paint is scooped up as it melts.

An electric sander or a sanding attachment on an ordinary power drill is also extremely effective, but very dusty. Great care needs to be taken to clear away all the dust, otherwise the tiny particles will show up in the new coat of paint. It is also important to wash the paintwork with hot, soapy water to remove any grease spots, which will show through both oil-and water-based paints.

During the preparations you may discover that the wood is rotten. This is a common problem with window frames. The wood is not only under attack from the elements outside, but condensation on the inside can also damage the frames. If the rot hasn't spread too far, it may be possible to replace spots of damaged timber with a wood filler, preferably one containing fibreglass which will allow the filler to adapt to any movement in the wood.

The window frame repair is quite a simple procedure. Gently dig out the rotten wood with either a chisel or a small scraper and clear away all loose pieces. Then apply the wood filler with a putty knife or scraper and smooth off. Don't worry if the surface is a little rough. When the filler is dry, rub down the area with glass paper for a smooth finish. The hardened filler makes an ideal painting surface.

When the window frame has been prepared, the final step is to stick masking tape around the windowpanes in case you catch the glass while painting. If the tape should end up heavily coated with paint, cut along the inside edge of the tape with a razor blade. This is to avoid pulling away any of the paint on the woodwork when the tape is ripped off.

For plasterwork, painted walls and ceilings need to be washed down to remove grease and dirt. Clean out any holes or cracks and plug them up with an appropriate filler. Rub down when dry. Preparing bare plaster for decorating is usually easy when it's in fairly good condition. The hard part comes when the walls have been covered with wallpaper which needs to come off in readiness for painting or for putting up new paper.

The cheapest but not necessarily the fastest way to strip a

wall involves soaking the paper with warm water and using a scraper to take it off. If the paper doesn't come away easily, give the wall an extra rinse down and leave for 10 minutes before attempting to have another go. Thick, textured papers are very thirsty and may require several dousings before they can be stripped. To remove waterproof papers, the surface needs to be scoured with either glass paper or an electric sander to enable the water to soak into the paper's backing.

A quicker way to remove wallpaper is to hire a steam stripper from a domestic plant hire firm or a do-it-yourself centre. They aren't difficult to operate. Cold water is poured into the stripper's tank and heated until the steam is pushed through a hose to a perforated headplate which is held against the wall. The steam loosens the paper and it comes away easily with a scraper.

If you are planning to put up new wallpaper, it's a good idea to coat or 'size' the walls with the recommended mixture of paste and water. This coating helps when sliding the lengths of paper into place and also stops the plaster absorbing paste from the paper.

Tools and techniques for painting

The size of the room and the materials you have chosen will, to a large extent, dictate the type of tools you're going to need. Brushes are used to paint both woodwork and plaster. Professional decorators consider brushes with natural bristles, such as hog hair, to be the best, because the strands retain more paint than manmade fibres. When money is tight it may be tempting to buy the cheapest brushes available, but such savings could turn out to be a false economy. A good brush will last for years, a poorly made one might start shedding its bristles as soon as you begin painting.

There is a wide range of brush sizes available to tackle both large and small painting projects. If you are planning to paint a wall, obviously go for a large size but not so big that it feels unwieldy. The standard 75 mm (3 in) brush is ideal for general woodwork such as doors and skirting boards and windowsills. Small brushes, 25 mm (1 in), or angled brushes are better suited for finer work such as the glazing bars in windows. There is even a brush with an extended handle called a crevice brush which makes it much easier to paint behind the radiators. However, a cheaper alternative is to tie a small brush to a long piece of wood.

Looking after your brush properly will extend its life. Emulsion paint can be washed out in soapy water, rinsing the brush in clear water afterwards. Oil-based paints are easily removed with turpentine or white spirit. Finally, never dry a brush in direct heat, otherwise the bristles will go stiff.

Whichever size brush you use, resist the temptation to apply the paint too thickly. To achieve a good finish, the undercoat and the top coat should be lightly applied. On large surfaces try to keep the painting edge wet, so that new paint flows in easily. But perhaps the most important part of painting is planning the order in which you will do it. Whether you are going to paint just one door or the whole room, the sequence is important. Knowing where to begin can help the novice painter achieve a more professional finish.

When painting a whole room, begin with the ceiling, then do the walls, then the windows and doors. Finish with the picture rails and skirting boards. Knowing where to begin on woodwork can also help the novice painter achieve a more professional finish. The general rule with panelled doors is to paint the mouldings first and work outwards. For doors with a smooth surface, start at the top and work down. By the time you've reached the bottom, you'll be able to see if the paint has run.

To minimise the likelihood of drips, lightly brush down after each section has been covered, then across, and finish off with an upward stroke. Professional decorators call this technique 'laying off'. But it isn't foolproof, so keep checking the newly painted surfaces every 15 minutes until they are virtually dry. Paint drips caught early enough can be smoothed down with a brush, but they soon harden and then they can only be removed by using fine glass paper and repainting.

If you have also painted the door's hinges, remember to move the door occasionally while the paint is drying. If you don't, the new coat will dry in a fixed position over the hinge's moving parts and is more likely to crack.

When painting window frames, start by tackling the moving parts first, for instance the back edge of a casement window, so that they will have all day to dry. If they are still wet when the window is closed, the paint will seal the two surfaces firmly together.

Rollers are generally used to paint large surfaces. Expensive rollers are made out of lambswool and mohair, but a cheaper alternative is foam. Most models have detachable roller heads, which helps with cleaning, and when the roller's surface is worn out, only the head needs to be replaced instead of the whole unit. You will also need a shallow tray thoroughly to coat the roller with paint. Try to avoid overloading the roller with paint; it will only slide off if you do. Gently run the roller over the paint in the tray until you have discovered how much the roller head can hold.

The one drawback to a roller is the 'splashback'. Tiny spots of paint are flicked off every now and again. But that's a small inconvenience when you consider that rollers cover large areas very quickly and can give a textured look to some plain walls. Keep a brush handy if the roller can't quite reach into some corners.

Paint pads are ideal for applying emulsion to walls and ceilings. Pads are also made out of either lambswool, mohair or foam and usually have detachable heads. They will last longer if they are cleaned straight after use. Be prepared to press and squeeze several times to make sure all the paint has been removed. Application methods for pads vary, but experienced painters tend to use light forward and backward strokes. Getting into corners is usually no problem.

Tools and techniques for wallpapering

To prepare wallpaper for hanging you are going to need a tape measure, to mark off the required lengths; a pair of wallpaper scissors, to cut the rolls of wallpaper and trim off the excess when fitting it; a paste brush and bucket with string tied across the mouth, to act as a rest for the brush; and a long table. There are special foldaway wallpaper tables on the market which when fully extended can measure around 185 cm (6 ft) in length. They aren't that expensive, but you could keep costs down by making one yourself. All you need are two sheets of hardboard measuring 61 cm (2 ft) in width and 93 cm (36$^{1}/_{2}$ in) in length, which are secured together with hinges. The hardboard top can then be laid across several pieces of furniture of roughly the same height. When it's not in use, it can be folded away.

When using patterned paper, the opening is usually the top, but not always, so read the manufacturers' instructions very carefully before cutting. Apply the paste to the middle of each strip and then work outwards to the edges (fig. 4.1). You will finish the job much quicker if you paste up several lengths at one go.

To prevent the glue drying, fold the strip into a kind of 'wallpaper parcel' (fig. 4.2). Gently lift the two end edges and bring them back so they meet in the middle of the length. The pasted sides are touching and won't quickly dry out. Crease back the two edges by about two inches so the paper can be held easily when it's being positioned against the wall.

Actually to hang the paper, you are going to need a step ladder; a plumb line, to doublecheck the paper is straight on the wall; a wallpaper brush, to smooth down the paper; and a cloth or sponge to wipe off excess paste. Finally, a pastry cutter. A what? It might sound unusual, but an ordinary pastry cutter is the ideal device for marking the cutting line. The wheel leaves tiny indentations which are easy to follow but not too obvious if you happen to make a mistake.

82 · *Setting up Home*

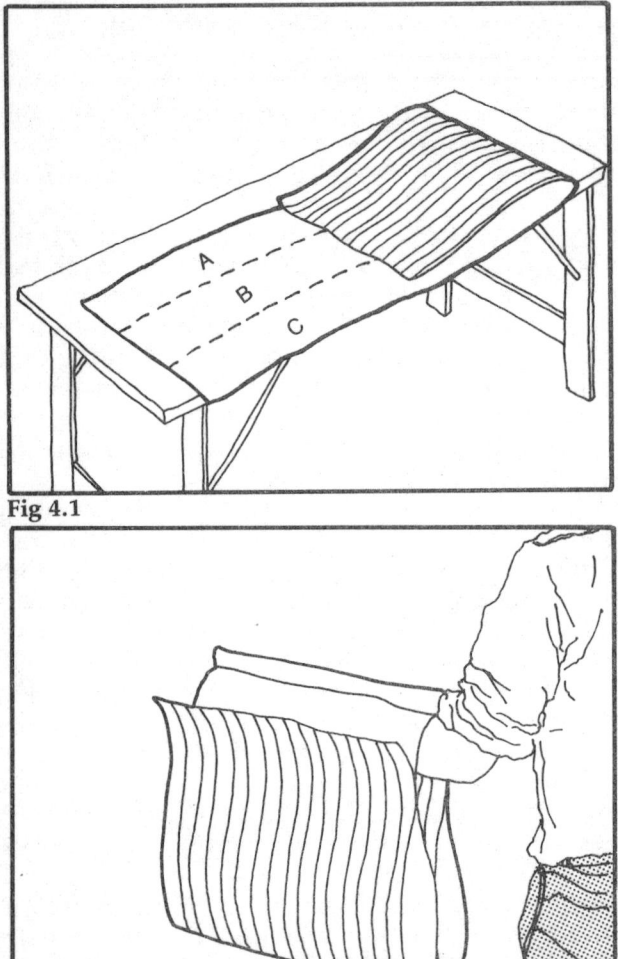

Fig 4.1

Fig 4.2

your level of expertise. The general rule with professional decorators is that you start from the main window in the room or from the fireplace if there is one (fig. 4.3). A beginner might feel happier tackling a straight line with no

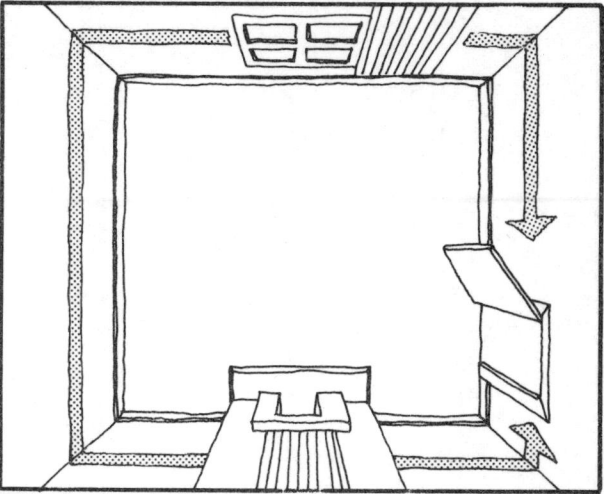

Fig 4.3

obstructions, until his or her confidence grows. Always cut the strips of paper longer than the space to be papered, as the lines of the ceiling and skirting board may not be straight and so need to be cut last, after the paper is stuck to the wall.

If you are tackling the job on your own, rest the wallpaper 'parcel' on one arm while you climb on a chair or step ladder. Begin by placing the paper so that it overlaps the ceiling join by about two inches. Slowly unfold it in two-feet sections then smooth on to the wall as you work down. This is only one suggested method; you may prefer to let the length of wallpaper hang loose while fitting it. If you do, make sure the paper doesn't rip in the middle. Remember, edges must only touch and not overlap.

When the whole strip is stuck down, crease along the line of the ceiling join with scissors and cut the excess off with a knife (fig 4.4). The same technique can be used at the bottom along the skirting board.

Hanging wallpaper is certainly easier when there are two people to manoeuvre the length into place. One person works from the top with the wallpaper brush while the

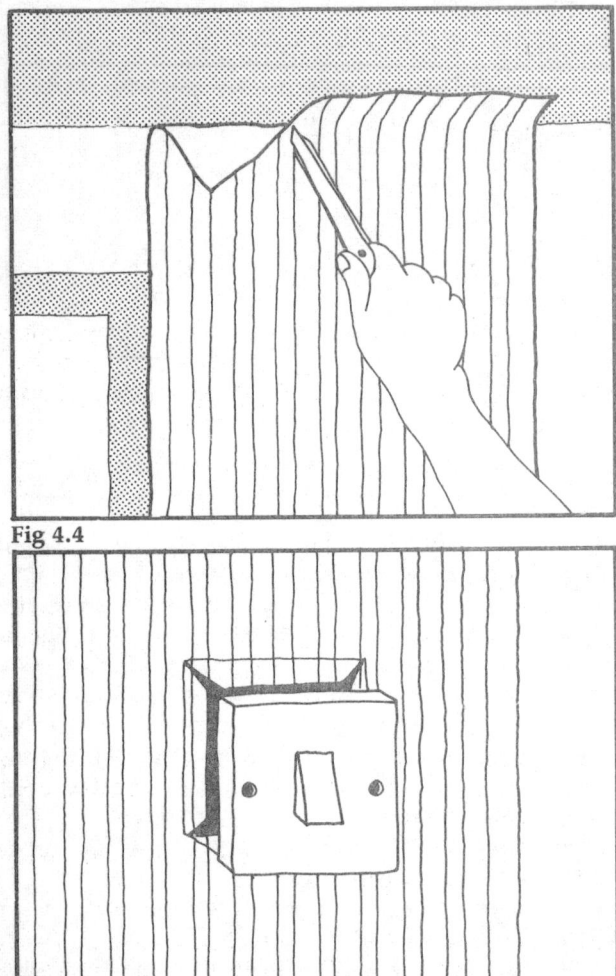

Fig 4.4

Fig 4.5

second aligns the paper. Common obstacles such as light switches can be marked with a cross and roughly cut out, but wait until the wallpaper is in place before fitting properly (fig. 4.5). Another good decorating tip is, don't try and take a large piece of wallpaper round a corner. Trim it so that there is just enough to go over the edge by about 25 mm (1 in).

Acquiring a few tricks of the trade should help you achieve less of an amateurish look and more of a professional finish.

DOING IT YOURSELF

Knowing how to deal with those everyday problems which arise, such as a leaking tap or a broken window, is an essential part of home ownership. Calling in a handyman or a plumber every time something goes wrong is going to be expensive. There's also the danger that you will become over-reliant on other people instead of developing a few basic DIY skills yourself. The last part of this chapter deals with some common problems which often crop up around the house and shows you how to fix them.

For a start, you should get yourself a basic tool kit. This does not have to be elaborate, but whatever you buy you should get the best you can afford, as these are the tools you will use most often. You can add to the basics as your interest and skills grow. Remember, it is not necessary to purchase expensive equipment which is rarely used, such as floor sanders or paper strippers, as these can be hired by the day when necessary.

The problem: broken window

Tools and materials: broad-bladed chisel, mallet, glass cutter, putty knife or an old 1-inch chisel, a pair of thick gloves, pane of glass, tub of putty and glazing sprigs or fine panel pins.

Protect your hands before attempting gently to tap out small pieces of glass from the top of the broken pane. Never start from the bottom in case a jagged piece of glass from the top drops on you. When all the glass has been removed, use the chisel to clear away any of the old putty. Be careful to avoid cutting into the timber.

Measure the width and length of the window frame and then deduct about 3 mm ($1/8$ in) from the measurements for the new glass. Glass can either be cut to size or you can trim it yourself. If you decide to do it yourself, make sure that the surface you cut on is flat and even. First cover the surface with a layer of newspapers or felt. Place the glass flat and mark the ends of the line you want to cut by nicking the edges with the glass cutter (fig 5.1). Clean the glass with turps and place a straight edge between the two nicks. Run the cutter along the edge. Don't be afraid to apply firm pressure (fig. 5.2). Now put the straight edge under the glass with one side along the scored line. Place one hand firmly on the glass over the straight edge and the other over the hanging side (fig. 5.3). Press down with both hands until the glass breaks. In all three steps the rule is firmness; too light and nervous a touch will result in broken glass much sooner than firmness and speed. If less than 6 mm ($1/4$ in) has to be removed, score a line with the glass cutter and use pliers to nibble the unwanted piece away.

Treat the newly exposed timber frame with primer and wait until it is dry before laying a line of putty. Rather than applying the putty straight from the tub on to the window frame, familiarise yourself with its texture by rolling the putty around in your hands. This will also make it easier to work with. If the putty does feel sticky, add a small quantity of plaster powder to achieve a better working consistency.

When you are ready, feed the putty through your forefinger and thumb on to the frame until the bedding of putty is about 10 mm (just under $1/2$ in) in thickness (fig. 6.1). Press the pane into the putty by applying pressure around the edges (fig. 6.2). Don't push too hard in the centre as it could crack the glass. When the pane is in place, use glazing sprigs or fine panel pins to firmly fix it in position (fig. 6.3). Put them into the frame so they are lying flat against the surface of the glass. Use the putty knife or chisel to make a smooth facing of about a 45° angle (fig. 6.4). Leave the putty for at least a

Decorating and do-it-yourself guide · **87**

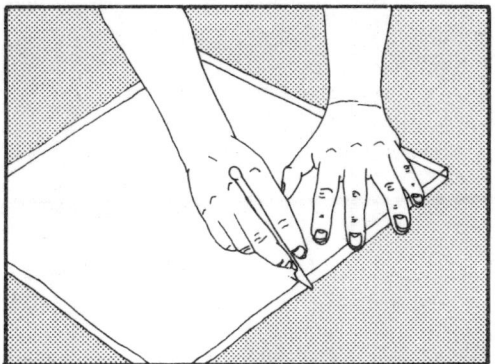

Fig 5.1

Fig 5.2

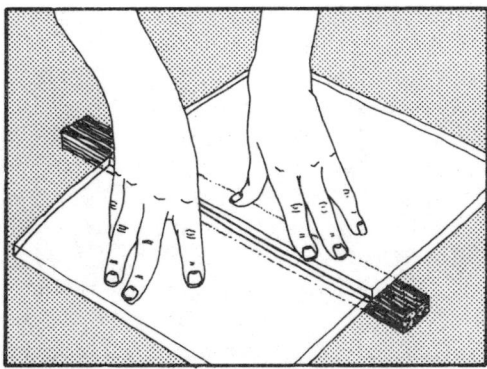

Fig 5.3

88 · Setting up Home

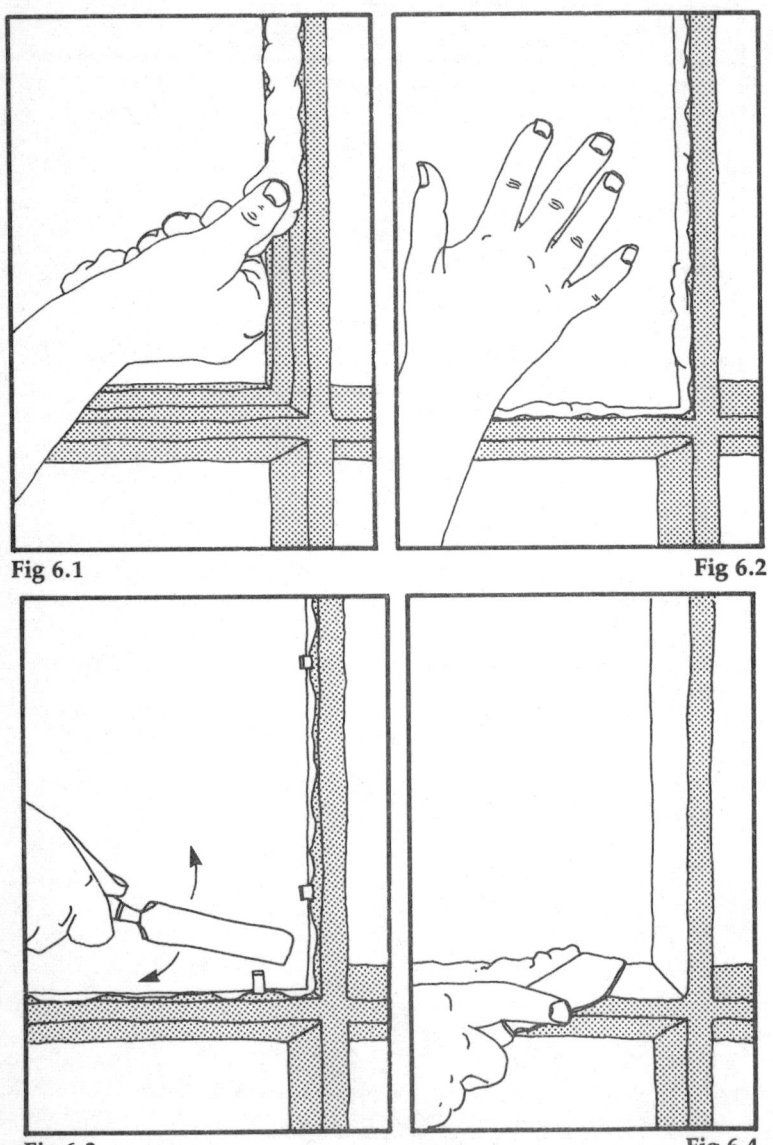

Fig 6.1

Fig 6.2

Fig 6.3

Fig 6.4

fortnight until the surface has hardened. Apply an oil-based primer before using an undercoat and gloss paint.

The problem: sticking doors or windows

Tools and materials: screwdriver, chisel, mallet, surform plane (open blade) and wooden wedge.

A door or window sometimes sticks because its hinge screws have worked loose. Check the hinges before attempting more drastic action.

If the wood has swollen, the only remedy is to plane one side of the problem window or door. Although it's not the easiest option, it is better to take shavings from the hinge side rather than cutting into the straight edge on show. If it's an outside door, it may have a mortice or rim lock fitted on the latter side.

Unscrew the hinges from the frame and then wedge the door or window securely between two chairs or a portable workbench before planing. If quite a bit of wood needs to be removed, the hinges will probably have to be resunk on the original sites. Go very gently with the plane: remember, it is easier to remove chippings than to put them back. Treat the newly exposed surface with wood sealer or varnish. If you don't, the wood will soak up moisture and swell again. When attempting to refit the door, use a wooden block as a support while tightening up the screws.

A door may also stick along its bottom. In this case, the problem may be solved by placing a piece of rough sandpaper under the door and closing it several times. If more is required, the door must be removed and planed as before.

If the door is sagging on its hinges, which usually means that it fails to close or squeaks as it moves, the first remedy is to tighten the screws in the hinges. If this fails, either replace the hinges with longer screws or insert small pieces of dowelling in the screw holes before refitting the old screws. Doors can also become hingebound if the screws on either side are too long, stopping the door from closing. Either tighten the screws or, if they still project, replace them with shorter ones.

The problem: faulty floorboards

Tools and materials: sandpaper, wood filler or papier mâché, stainer, brads, hammer, talcum powder, plane, saw, chisel.

Most houses in Britain still have tongue and groove floorboards, though in many modern apartment blocks this is no longer the case. With time and wear floorboards can become loose, warped, or start to creak when stepped upon. All these problems can be overcome quite easily by anyone with a little common sense. However, more serious problems such as sinking floorboards, which are usually caused by faulty joists, may require more expert skills. If you are a real DIY enthusiast, it is worth looking under the floorboards to check the condition of the joists. If they are free of fungus and other infections it may be possible simply to bolt an extra piece of wood as a strengthener on to the offending joist, but make sure that the top of the strengthener does not poke above the top of the joist. However, if the joists have been rotted by an infection, you should get a specialist in to look at them.

Another common floor problem is gaps. Shrinking is the most usual cause of gaps appearing between floorboards, though they can also be caused by pests or diseases in the wood. If the boards are infested, they must be replaced in part or in whole; but if the boards are healthy, small holes can be filled with wood filler or with a papier mâché mix of pulped newspaper and thick wallpaper paste. Simply sandpaper the filler smooth when dry. If the boards are exposed, an appropriate stainer can be mixed with the papier mâché to blend it in with the natural wood tone. If the holes are really large, pieces of wood can be hammered in to fill the gap, but a floor with many large gaps will need to be relaid entirely or covered over with hardboard.

If you have loose or creaking floorboards, the first remedy

Decorating and do-it-yourself guide · 91

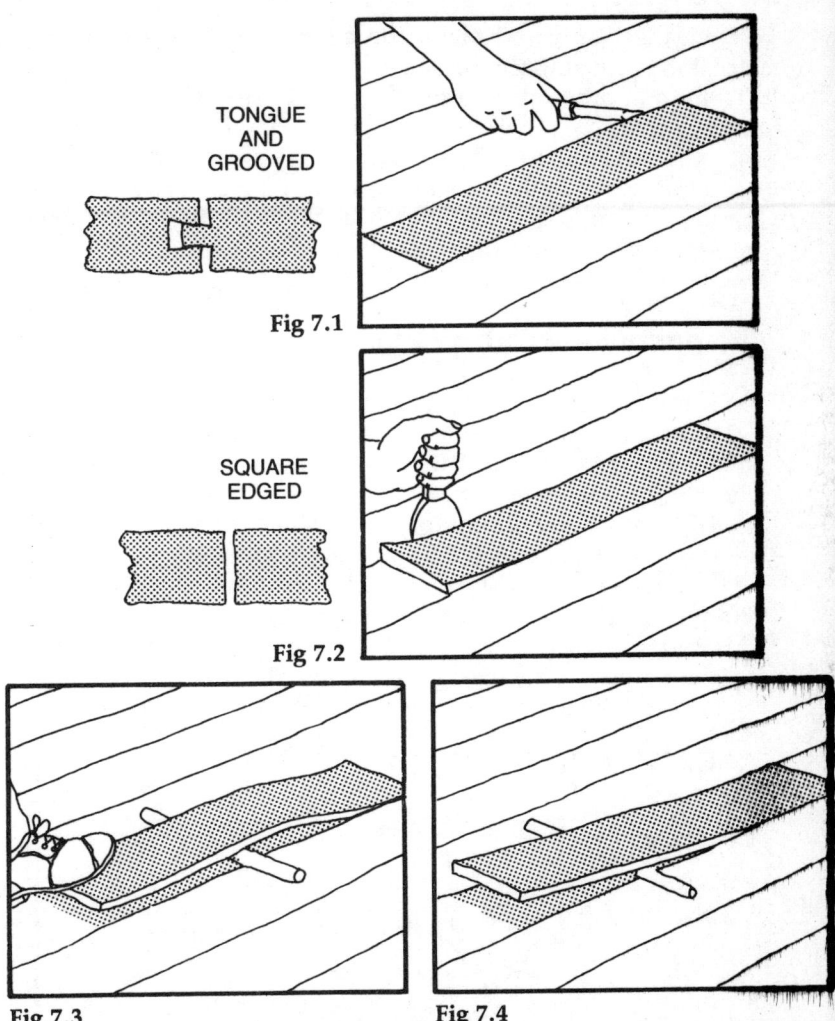

TONGUE AND GROOVED

Fig 7.1

SQUARE EDGED

Fig 7.2

Fig 7.3

Fig 7.4

is to try nailing new brads close to the existing ones. **Brads** are the special nails used to hold floorboards down. **Creaking** often occurs because the brads have become loose in **the** boards. If creaking or looseness persists, try dusting **talcum** powder into the cracks. When all else fails you will have **to** remove the board and plane the edge to remove whatever extrusion is causing the noise.

To lift a floorboard, you must first cut through the tongue on one side (fig. 7.1). Then, using a chisel as a lever, you can prize one end up (fig. 7.2). Next, insert an iron rod under the board (fig. 7.3) and, using your foot, press down on the loose end so that now the other end will be pushed up by the pressure from the rod (fig. 7.4).

The problem: weathered mortar

Tools and materials: plugging chisel, pointing trowel, bucket and spade, cement and sharp or building sand.

Exposure to the elements can take its toll, particularly where mortar is being repeatedly splashed with water, such as at the mouth of a drainpipe. Rain water gushes down and is often flung back as it hits the grille over a drain.

Don't make the mistake of trying to apply new mortar before properly preparing the surface. Scrape out about 13 to 20 mm (between $^1/_2$ and $^3/_4$ in) of the old, crumbling cement by using a plugging chisel. The angled blade is ideal for this type of work. The next stage is to mix up a mortar mixture of

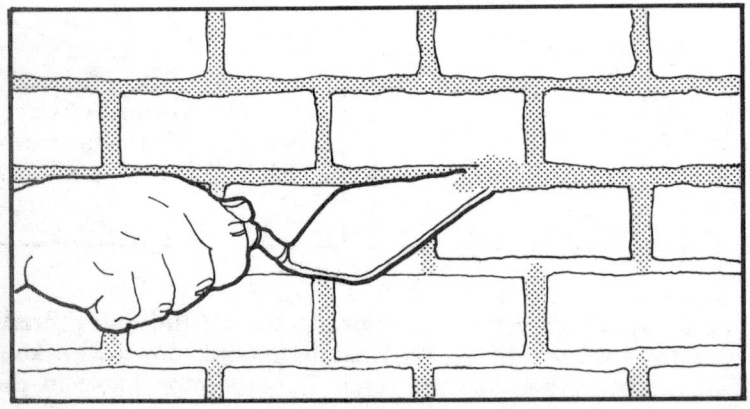

Fig 8

one part cement and three parts sand. For rendering repairs around drain areas, use sharp or plastering sand as it is less likely to crack up in wet conditions; otherwise buy building sand. Mix the sand and cement before adding clean water. If the weather is frosty when you are trying to mix your mortar, add a little builder's anti-freeze to the water to improve the cement's working consistency.

Apply the mortar with a pointing trowel along the vertical gaps first (fig. 8). The trowel is useful in creating a downward angle in the line of mortar. When the rain hits the brickwork the water then runs straight off. This slight angle will minimise the weathering effects of the rain, as will a tile or slate propped up behind the drainpipe. The water splashes then hit the tile and not the wall.

The problem: leaking tap

Tools and materials: small wrench, spanner, screwdriver and new washer.

The drip, drip, drip of a leaking tap is often the sign that the washer needs replacing. A washer is a ring-shaped device which makes a watertight seal when working properly. For a standard kitchen tap the most common size is 15 mm ($^1/_2$ in) with 22 mm ($^3/_4$ in) for bath taps.

Before attempting to dismantle the tap, make sure the water supply has been turned off and the system is drained. The mains stopcock tends to be downstairs under or by the kitchen sink, but it can sometimes be outside in the road. Don't leave any water heaters on while the system is empty.

The screw to release the tap's head is either at the side or hidden under the centre disc. Fasten a wrench around the main body of the tap to hold it steady while the cover is taken off. Underneath will be a large nut, the gland nut, which holds the headgear in place. Loosen the nut with a spanner and lift off (fig. 9). The washer sits on a part called the jumper. When the tap is turned on, the jumper moves up and allows the water to flow. The washer is often attached to

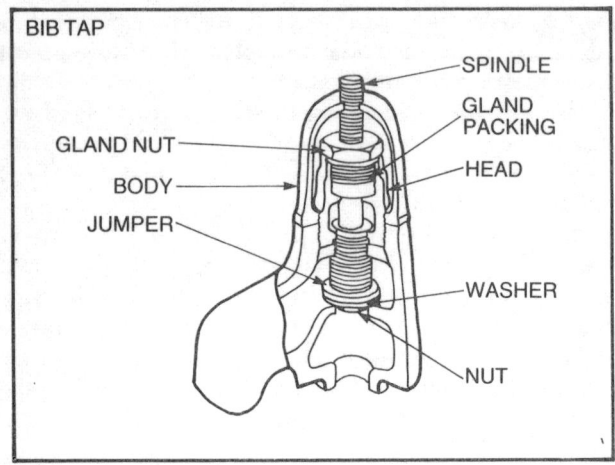

Fig 9

the jumper by a brass nut. Unscrew the nut with your fingers or a spanner, put the new washer in place and reassemble the tap. See – easy when you know how.

The problem: running overflow

Tools and materials: pliers, mole grip wrench, torch, bent nail or screwdriver, new valve washer or ball float.

In the standard ball valve system the two common causes of a running overflow are a punctured ball float or a worn washer. When the ball has become waterlogged it will sink. The water won't be shut off and will continue to fill up the tank and overflow. The ball float is normally just screwed on to the lever arm and is easy to replace.

Putting in a new washer is a more complicated procedure and requires the water supply to be turned off. The lever arm is held in place by a split pin. Take out the pin by first closing its two arms with a set of pliers. Then remove the arm from the piston. On some cylinders the cap end has to be taken off before the piston can be removed from the ball valve with the aid of a bent nail or wire. Hold the piston body with mole grips and turn the removable section anti-clockwise with pliers. Open up and take out the faulty washer, put in the replacement and reassemble.

The problem: blocked sink, basin or bath

Tools and materials: soda crystals, plastic plunger, flexible metal rod, spanner, rubber gloves, bucket and a piece of wire.

The tools listed above represent those needed for four different methods of clearing a blocked sink. Hopefully, you won't need them all.

- *Remedy number one.* If a blockage has been caused by a build-up of grease deposits in the drain, a generous amount of soda crystals dissolved in boiling water will do the trick. Protect your hands with rubber gloves before handling the soda crystals.
- *Remedy number two.* This involves the plastic plunger and a spot of elbow grease. Place the plunger over the plughole and run a little water into the sink. Work the plunger. The pressure on the plunger is sometimes enough to dislodge the blockage.
- *Remedy number three.* A flexible rod is really a long strip of metal, pointed and weighted at one end. The rod is inserted through the plughole and its head is lowered down the drain until it meets the obstruction and is pushed through.
- *Remedy number four.* In order to get into the pipe you will have to open it somewhere in the trap. The trap is the bent part of the pipe which prevents foul air from entering the house from the drains (fig. 10). The access point may be a small plug which can be twisted off with a spanner, a plastic band holding the two sections

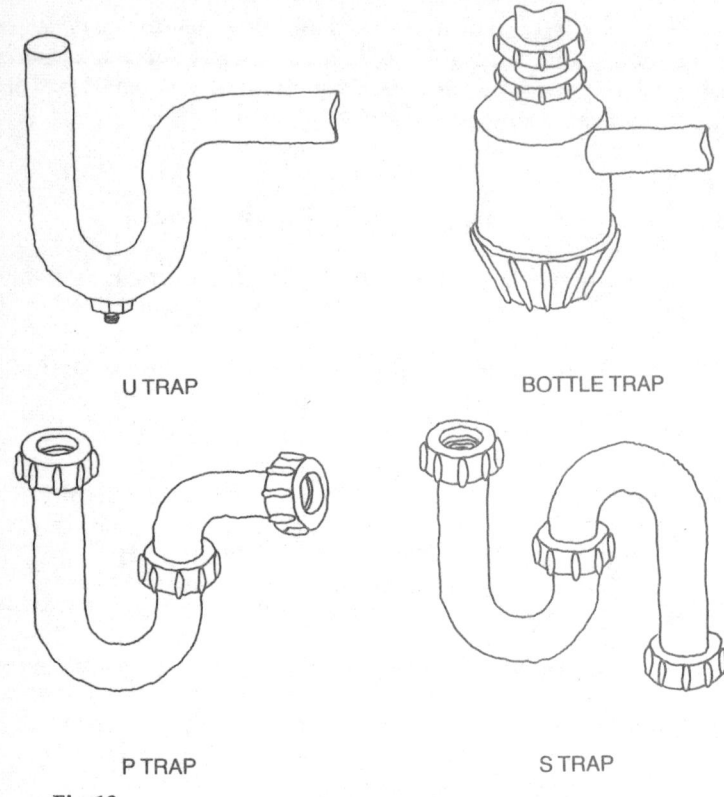

Fig 10

together, or a simple cap-like device. This will depend on what type of trap you have. The illustrations should help you to identify what your type of pipe is. Once you have found the point of entry, place a bucket in position under it, open the trap and, using a piece of wire, fish around inside the drain. To prevent grease deposits building up in the future, regularly swill with boiling water and soda crystals to keep your drains clean. Note, however, that although using soda is a good way to keep your pipes clean in general or to unblock slightly clogged pipes, it should not be used if the blockage is complete. In this case you should call in a specialist.

The problem: leaking guttering or drainpipes

Tools and materials: scissors or a sharp knife, flash band, blow-torch, ladder and wire brush.

Replacing a length of guttering or a drainpipe can be an expensive business. A cheaper alternative is to cover the hole with a piece of flash band, an aluminium-based strip with an adhesive backing.

First clean around the crack with a wire brush to remove any loose flakes of metal or paint. Measure the repair and add on at least 18 cm (about 5 in) so that the flash band is attached to a firm base. Heat the cut strip with a blow-torch until it becomes flexible and easier to work with. Then place the adhesive side over the rupture and smooth into place. The strip dries quickly and can be painted over. At a distance the repair will be difficult to detect and, although the flash band is only a temporary measure, it can last for several years.

Regular maintenance work is the best deterrent against cracks forming in metal gutterings and drainpipes. Paint offers some protection, so check if there is any exposed metal which has started to rust. The backs of drainpipes are particularly susceptible, as they are often missed when the pipes were last painted. Gutterings should also be regularly cleaned, especially in the autumn when leaves are falling. If leaves are allowed to clog up the gutters, the water will overflow and cause damp patches on the brickwork as well as soaking through to the inside walls.

If a gutter continues to overflow after cleaning, then it may be sagging. The problem is usually due to a broken bracket or loosened screws. The solution is simply to replace the bracket as close to the old one as possible. It is sometimes possible to remedy a sagging gutter by placing a small piece of wood between the gutter and the bracket, but this should only be regarded as a temporary solution.

The problem: ill-fitting window frames

Tools and materials: mastic-based filler and applicator gun.

When there is a small space between the window frames and the brickwork, use a mastic product to fill up the gap. This type of filler material doesn't become rigid and is therefore able to adjust to any movement of the frame. The filler is usually sold in tubes with a long nozzle. The applicator gun is fixed to the tube's movable base and is used to push the filler slowly out. Where you snip the nozzle will determine the thickness of the squeezed-out filler. During application, make sure the tip of the nozzle touches both sides and, if the filler needs to be smoothed down, use a wet, round-bladed knife.

The problem: peeling window frames

Tools and materials: glass paper, primer and flash band, scissors, blow lamp and paint scraper.

The high level of sunshine on a south-facing wall can cause painted surfaces to peel. To avoid having to repaint every six months, cover the wood with flash band and then paint over it. The wood's surface needs to be sanded down and coated with special flash band primer, because the timber is porous, before placing the previously warmed adhesive strip to the wood.

If the wood has to be stripped of old paint before coating again, the quickest way is to use a blow lamp. Hold the nozzle about five or six inches away from the surface, and always keep the flame moving to prevent wood from charring. When the paint begins to melt, scrape off with the paint scraper, working in the direction of the grain. There are some problems using a blow lamp, as glass can crack if it gets too heated and there is always the danger of fire. If you are wary of fire, a hot-air gun, which works like a large hairdryer, will do the job just as effectively. There are numerous chemical solvents which can also be used to melt paint before it is scraped of. These same stripping techniques can also be used on larger areas such as doors and walls.

The problem: cracks and holes in plaster

Tools and materials: paint scraper, brush or water spray, bucket, plaster/filler.

Inside walls may be of four types: solid walls with plaster coated directly on to brickwork (fig. 11.1); plaster and lath walls, which are made by laying plaster over a framework of narrow wooden laths tacked on to the wooden studs which support the wall (fig. 11.2); dry-lined walls, which are made of plasterboard nailed on to masonry (fig. 11.3); and partition walls, which are made of two layers of plasterboard nailed to

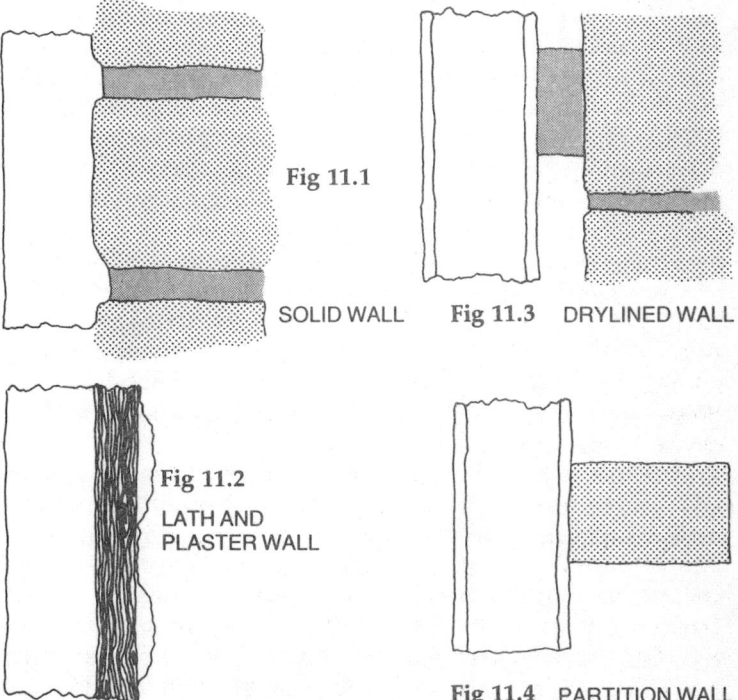

Fig 11.1 SOLID WALL

Fig 11.3 DRYLINED WALL

Fig 11.2 LATH AND PLASTER WALL

Fig 11.4 PARTITION WALL

the internal studs (fig. 11.4). These last walls are completely hollow, and it is very difficult to attach any objects to them unless you put the nail into the part of the wall where the studs are. You should be able to tell where these are by the nails already present. If you are in doubt as to which type of wall you have, you will have to drill a hole in an inconspicuous spot to determine what your wall is made of.

If you have long, straight, hairline cracks this is probably caused by movement of plasterboards, in which case it is useless to fill them, as the plaster will only drop out again. Covering over with textured paper is the best solution. Similarly with cracks in the plaster between the walls and the ceiling, which are caused by movements of the house. Long, wide, vertical cracks probably indicate a serious structural fault and should be examined by a builder. However, small holes in plaster and plasterboard can be repaired easily.

With holes in plaster walls, simply remove the loose plaster with a knife until you have a hole with solid sides (fig. 12.1). Try to cut the plaster below the edges of the hole in from the top surface, so that the new plaster will lay in more firmly. Brush away all dust and dampen all the sides of the hole and the exposed wall by painting with a wet paintbrush or spraying with a plant water-sprayer before plastering (fig. 12.2). Mix the filler as directed on the packet and press into the damaged area with the paint scraper (fig. 12.3). Remove excess filler by drawing the flat edge over the surface when the hole is full. With deep holes you may have to apply two layers, as the first may dribble down before the plaster sets if too thick a layer is applied in one go. When dry, sand the surface with glass paper (fig. 12.4). A variety of cellulose fillers are available in powder form, for mixing with water, or in ready-to-use form. You should choose your product according to the type of hole. The same procedure may be applied to relatively large holes in plaster walls and ceilings. But again, these may need several coats.

If the wall is made of plasterboard and the hole is small, the same procedure may be used. If the hole is larger, however, it is best to cut out the damaged area and replace

Decorating and do-it-yourself guide · 101

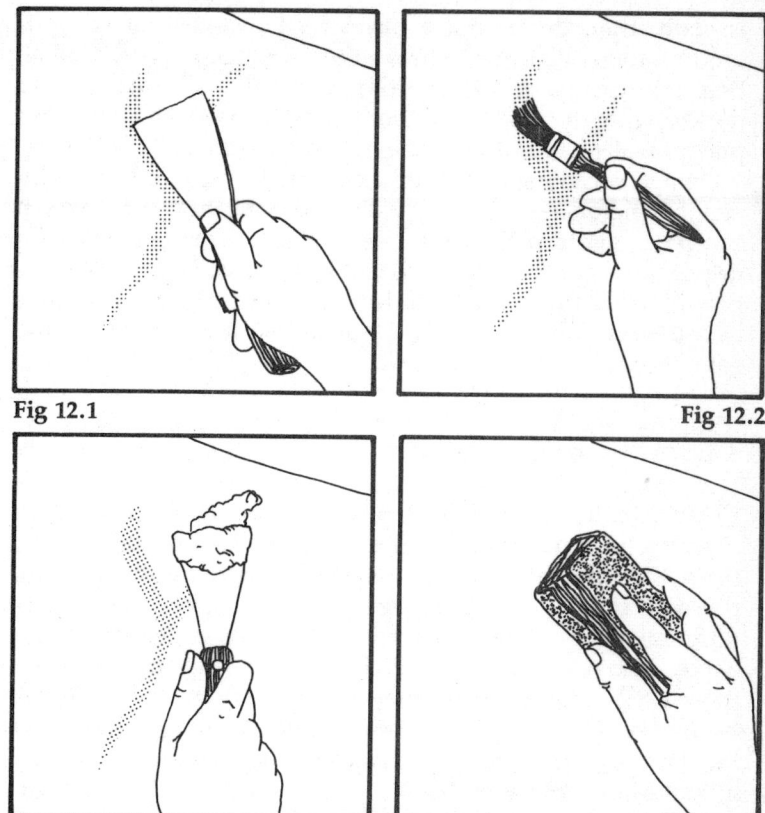

Fig 12.1

Fig 12.2

Fig 12.3

Fig 12.4

it with a similarly shaped piece of board which is nailed into the joists. The edges can then be covered over as above.

Apart from repairs to your house, there are also many decorative jobs which it is possible to do yourself.

The job: wall fixings

Tools and materials: hammer or screwdriver.

Mirrors, pictures, coat hooks: There always seems to be something which needs to be fixed to a wall. If your wall is solid, then this is not a problem. However, many walls are not solid. Figure 11 shows the four main types of wall. Before deciding to fix anything to your wall, you should decide what type it is, as both plasterboard and lath and plaster walls will not take heavy fixings easily.

Fixings vary from self-adhesive pads for holding lightweight pictures to strong walls, to masonry nails which can be driven directly into solid walls, to spring toggles for gripping to hollow walls and ceilings. Rawlplugs, which are plastic tubes fitted into a hole drilled in the wall, also give added strength in gripping the nail or screw put in to hold something.

The job: curtains

Curtains add warmth and beauty to a room, as well as blocking out undesirable views and protecting privacy. Apart from the choice of fabric and the length of the curtain, the rail must also be chosen carefully. There are many different types of rail, and these days most people choose a plastic track rather than a heavy rod, as curtains move more easily on tracks and they can be bent around corners if necessary. If you choose to have heavy curtains, you should buy overlapping tracks which allow the curtains to overlap about six inches when drawn.

The job: shelving

It is surprising how many things people begin to accumulate when they have their own home. Shelves are one of the most practical ways of providing a space for things to live on, as they offer instant access to the items stored there while also providing a place to display more decorative pieces. Shelves can be built in existing cupboards, in wall recesses such as on either side of the fireplace, or on plain walls in any room of the house.

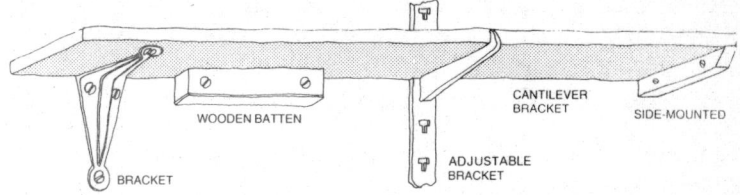

Fig 13

Basically there are two types of shelving: wall-mounted, where the battens or brackets are attached to the wall along which the shelf runs, and side-mounted, where the battens or brackets are attached to the ends of the shelves along a wall perpendicular to the shelf itself (fig. 13). For *very* heavy loads, you should put brackets or battens at both ends and in the middle. Shelves may be fixed directly to the wall or may be part of an adjustable system. The advantage of systems is that new shelves can be added or old ones moved at any time, as your needs change. Whatever type of shelf you choose, make sure that the fixing you use is strong enough for the wall and to take the load it will have to bear, which includes the weight of the shelf itself plus whatever is to be put on it.

There are a number of different types of support you can use for your shelves (fig. 13). For the shelves themselves you can use wood or glass. Glass is excellent for showing off special items or in the bathroom, but it cannot be used for heavy loads. The most popular type of wood is chipboard, because it is cheap and comes in a variety of finishes. However, it is not as strong as other woods and therefore requires more brackets. Plywood is also suitable.

The job: laying floor coverings

Tools: scriber (wooden block with a protruding nail), ruler, Stanley knife, adhesive as per instructions.

These days there is an enormous variety of floor coverings

104 · Setting up Home

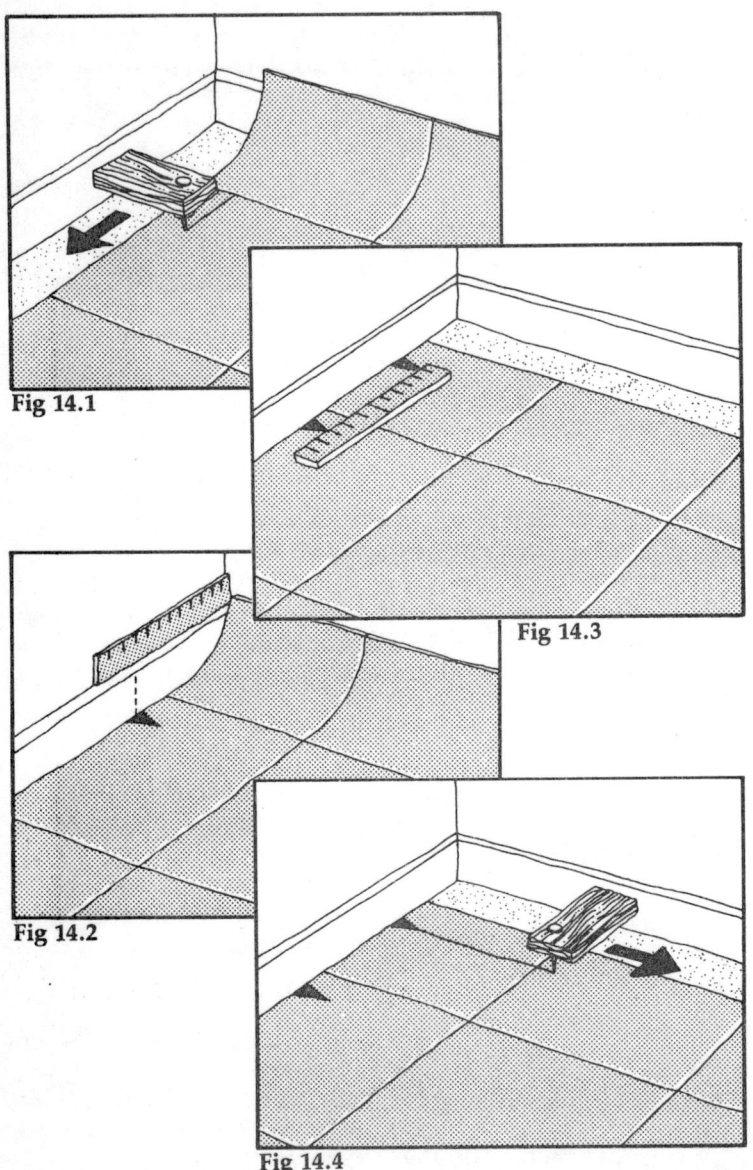

Fig 14.1

Fig 14.3

Fig 14.2

Fig 14.4

available, ranging from stone to vinyl. Difficult jobs such as quarry tiles should be left to an expert, but many coverings such as cork or vinyl sheeting are relatively easy to lay.

When buying your covering, buy about 5 per cent more than the measured area of the room, more if the pattern is large, as matching up the pattern often causes quite a bit of wastage. Both vinyl and cork need to be laid out flat for about two days to allow for settling before you fit them into place.

In order to cut the sheeting so that it fits the room exactly, place the strip about two inches from a side wall, leaving about three inches extra at each end. Run the scriber along the side wall, marking the sheeting (fig. 14.1). Cut along this line with the knife. Now push the strip up to the wall and it should fit exactly. Next, measure 10 inches from the end wall and mark the edge of the sheet with a pen (fig. 14.2). Pull the sheet so that the end is about two inches away from the wall and lying flat on the floor (fig. 14.3). Measure 10 inches back from the original pen mark. Now run the scriber along the end wall starting at the second mark and cut along the line (fig. 14.4). The sheet should now fit exactly at both the side and the end. Repeat the process from the start for the other end and follow the same procedure for all other strips.

The job: wiring a plug

Tools: pliers or knife, screwdriver.

One of the simplest and most frequently required household maintenance jobs is wiring a plug, but it is surprising how many people have never done it. There is absolutely nothing to be afraid of when wiring a plug, as long as the appliance is not connected to any supply of electricity and you connect the wires to the correct terminals.

The standard flex, the cable which carries the electricity from the plug to the appliance, is called three-core because it has three wires inside. Three-core flex comes in a variety of types, but all are colour-coded so that you can always be sure which wire is which (fig. 15.1). Two-core flex is also available for doubly insulated appliances, but should not be used on ordinary appliances (fig. 15.2). In general, in all types of flex the live is brown, or red in the old type (fig. 15.3), the neutral is blue, and the earth is green or green striped.

When wiring a plug, the most important point to remember is to attach the right wire to the right terminal. If you have a new plug, the paper cover over the plug will tell you which colour wire goes to which terminal. If your plug is old, you should note the positioning of the old wires before you remove them. After unscrewing the cover of the plug and removing the old fuse, carefully cut away the outer covering of the flex to about two inches using a knife or pliers. Insert the flex under the clamp and open the wires out (fig. 16.1). Cut back the plastic from the wires about half an inch, or whatever

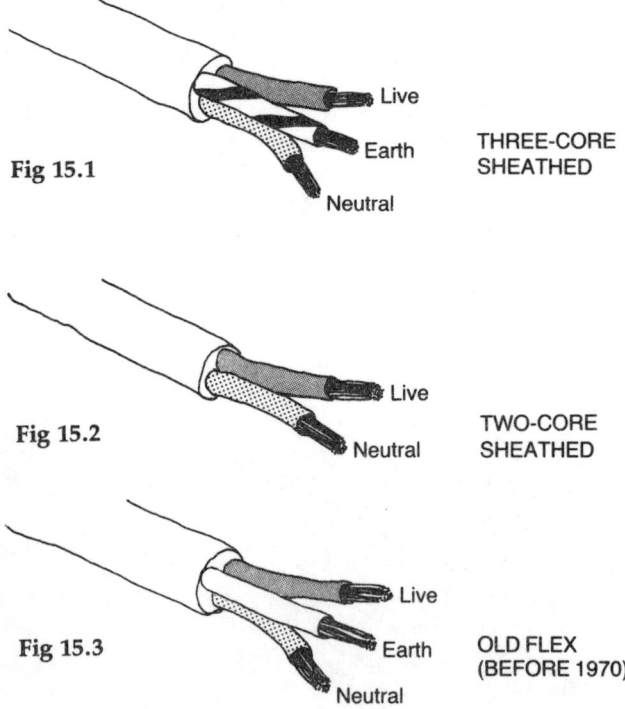

Fig 15.1 — THREE-CORE SHEATHED

Fig 15.2 — TWO-CORE SHEATHED

Fig 15.3 — OLD FLEX (BEFORE 1970)

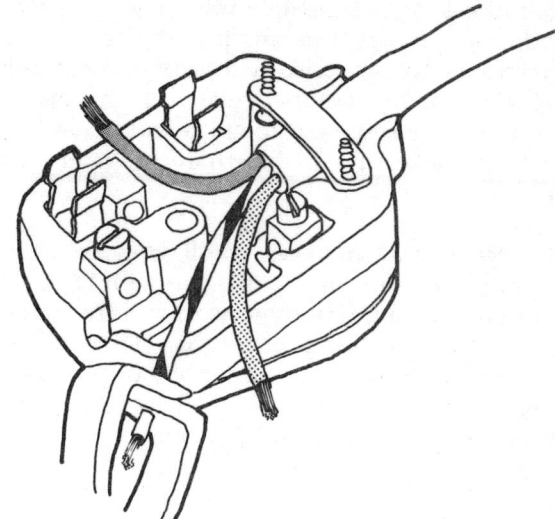

Fig 16.1

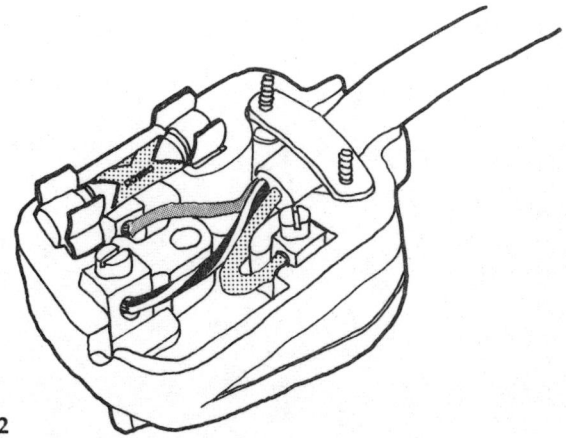

Fig 16.2

is required to get them to lie flat in the plug. Twist each wire end together and insert the ends into the correct terminals. Make sure there are no loose wire strands protruding (fig. 16.2). Tighten up the terminal screws, fit a new fuse and replace the cover. Remember to check you have the correct gauge of fuse. Never use higher than the gauge already in the plug.

After you have done it once, you'll wonder why it ever seemed so difficult. But this is the rule with DIY. The more you do, the more confidence you gain and the less daunted you will feel about tackling new jobs. Doing it yourself is not only money-saving, it can also give you a great sense of achievement and, because you did it yourself, help to make you feel that this house is truly your home.

7
Gardening and other hobbies

Moving into a place of your own opens the door to many home-based hobbies which you might not have tried before, perhaps through lack of space or even incentive. Some hobbies, such as gardening, may actually increase the value of your property, while upholstery will provide additional home comforts. Whether the new interest is taken up for pleasure, necessity or financial gain, give careful consideration to the following four factors.

- *Investment.* How expensive is starting up going to be, and what are the running costs?

- *Tuition.* Is it possible to gain expertise through a step-by-step guide, or will the hobby require instruction from a private tutor or a night school class?

- *Commitment.* How much time and effort will the new interest demand, and does that correspond with how much you are willing to give?

- *Storage.* If there is equipment involved, what storage space is going to be required?

By carefully working out all the pros and cons, you stand a better chance of picking a hobby tailor-made for your pocket, your needs and your skills.

OUTDOOR GARDENING

This can be extremely satisfying and productive, and is likely to make your home a more attractive proposition if or when you decide to put it on the market. A good gardener makes the most of what he or she has, whether it's an acre of land or a backyard with a lawn the size of a tablecloth.

Success is cultivated by having a thorough knowledge of the growing conditions in your garden. Only then is it possible to assess which varieties of plant are going to do well. The term 'growing conditions' encompass geographic position, i.e. in which part of the country you live (it's generally a colder climate in the north of Scotland than in the south of England), the level of shade and sunlight in the garden, and the type of soil and its condition.

If you thought soil was just dirt which stuck to your wellington boots, think again. Soil is made up of minerals and organic matter. The different combinations produce different types for growing purposes.

- *Chalky soil.* This is white and requires 'mulching', that is, forking in garden compost or manure for nutrients.

- *Clay soil.* This clings in lumps to the spade and footwear when wet. Often red in colour and very poor for drainage.

- *Peat soil.* This is generally quite dark and feels springy underfoot. Found mostly in the east of England.

- *Sandy soil.* This dries out very quickly and requires plenty of peat.

A soil's texture is determined by three materials: clay, sand and silt. Too much of one will cause an imbalance and present problems. (See above.) The ideal is to aim for a fairly even mix of all three to create a more balanced type of soil.

Owners of newly built homes should excavate 18 cm (7 in) to check that the builders haven't simply laid a dressing of soil on top of their building rubble. The only remedy is to import enough soil or loam to cover the garden to a depth of approximately 30 to 46 cm (about 12 to 18 in).

After working out the type of soil you have, the next step is to consider if anything needs to be added to improve its condition. Soil-testing kits are available at most garden centres. They will reveal whether a soil is acidic or alkaline, and if it requires treatment. This is called the pH condition of the soil.

Flora

Buying new stock can be an expensive business, so whether a whole new design is envisaged or just a few cosmetic changes, a visit to the local garden centre will give you a good idea of prices. A little window shopping may prevent you planning for more than you can afford.

Trying to work out which varieties to include in the garden can be confusing if the names given to different groups are unclear. For instance, an annual plant completes its cycle in one season. It grows from seed to flowering plant then dies. A biennial takes two years to reach maturity. In the first season the seed will produce root growth and foliage, but the flowers won't bloom until the following year. If a shrub is described as hardy, it is safe to plant outside, but if a variety is described as half-hardy then the seeds must be grown inside until there is no longer any risk of frosts, and then transplanted outside. Most good garden centres clearly label their plants and shrubs, and should also give some indication of the height they will reach when mature.

While you are trying to decide what to plant, take a discreet look at the gardens around your area. The shrubs and so on which thrive for the neighbours should also grow well for you. Consider how they have laid out their gardens. Are there any features which could be incorporated into your garden?

Planning a garden

Take some measurements in the garden and work out a suitable scale to help maintain a proper perspective while drawing. Sketch the old garden on a plain piece of paper and indicate which direction is south. Discreetly shade in the parts which don't receive much sun. Lay on top of the scaled diagram a piece of tracing or greaseproof paper. Draw your own garden plan on this sheet so that you can see at a glance which of the original features will be included or excluded in the new design (fig. 17).

The art of the landscape gardener lies in successfully blending practical considerations with aesthetic appeal. One school of thought believes that a garden should reflect the age of the property rather than be too loud and brash.

A common mistake many novice gardeners make is to over-plant. Borders and rockeries are filled to overflowing with new plants, and when they reach maturity there isn't enough room for them all. To avoid serious overcrowding, accept that initially new borders might have to look a little sparse until the plants and shrubs mature.

The same rule applies when planting trees. Allow enough space for them to grow and don't site them too close to your property, as their roots can cause damage to the foundations. Trees and larger shrubs can be used to form a windbreak in an exposed area of your garden or act as a boundary between your property and the neighbours'. Straight lines and corners can be broken up or disguised by the subtle use of borders and rockeries. A crazy-paving path can be constructed around your lawn and creates an impression of age.

Planting a herb garden

The most commonly used herbs such as sage, thyme, oregano, chives, fennel and parsley thrive in direct sunshine. An ideal place for a herb garden is a nice, warm spot as near as possible to the kitchen door. No busy cook fancies a trek down to the bottom of the garden every time he or she wants a sprig of mint.

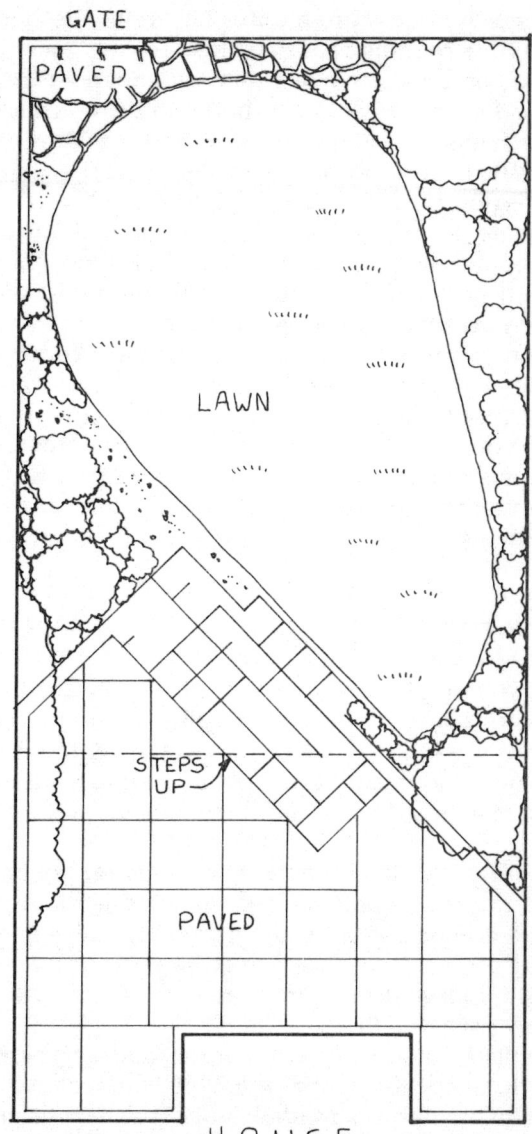

Fig 17

When space is at a premium, plant only the herbs most suited to your cooking requirements. Thyme goes well with stews and casseroles, while rosemary enhances the flavour of lamb. After deciding which herbs to grow, check on the height each plant is likely to reach when mature, to avoid taller varieties overshadowing smaller ones.

Even if your garden comprises just a small yard, you can still cultivate a herb patch. Why not grow them in plastic troughs or terracotta pots? In fact, mint should always be grown in a pot, as otherwise its roots will infest the rest of the garden because it grows so rampantly.

There are many varieties of mint, the most common being spearmint. The eau-de-cologne mint has pretty leaves and a lovely perfume. Herbs are often very attractive plants: not only can you create a sweet-smelling herb garden but also one which is a floral attraction in its own right. Rosemary is scented and produces little blue flowers, while fennel flowers are a pretty yellow.

Window-boxes

Gardening can take many forms, so if you are living in a flat with no patch of earth to call your own, have you considered a window-box? Good garden centres and shops stock them, and many come as a complete kit including brackets, masonry screws and rawlplugs to fix the box to the wall.

The do-it-yourself enthusiasts may prefer to build their own. An important point to bear in mind is that a window-box is only as good as its weatherproofing. Be generous with the wood preservative, use galvanised rather than ordinary nails, and make sure there's adequate drainage or your plants will rot.

Small plants such as salvia, pansies and geraniums all do well in the window-box which is well watered and well fed. Don't rely on natural rainfall when the box is in a very sheltered spot.

INDOOR GARDENING

The key to success with indoor gardening lies in selecting plants which are going to thrive in your home conditions. Keeping greenery indoors only becomes a hit-and-miss affair when the plants are purchased without any knowledge of their growing requirements and are killed off because what proved to be their final resting place was chosen through ignorance. A plant will only flourish if the environment is right; the same rule applies both indoors and out.

Test the temperatures around your home before buying anything. Even with radiators there can be quite a range: 21 °C (70 °F) in living-rooms, 18 °C (65 °F) in bathrooms and 15 °C (60 °F) in bedrooms. Plants which enjoy warm conditions, such as geraniums, busy lizzies and begonias, may vary in whether they need direct or indirect sunlight. Geraniums prefer a sunny south-facing windowsill, but busy lizzies and begonias are happier set back a little. When you actually buy your plants, be specific and ask about temperature and whether the plant should be housed in or out of direct sunshine. Find out how often it needs to be watered and fed.

Most good garden centres and shops have quite a wide selection of stock, from cactus to cyclamen. Many gardeners also find tempting bargains on the local market stall. Wherever you shop, take nothing at face value. Look closely for any signs of infestation such as greenfly or the red spider mite, which is a tiny, tiny pest found on the underside of leaves and can quickly spread to other plants.

Although plants can be brought into the house at any time of year, their feeding and watering requirements are going to vary depending on the season. Inexperienced gardeners often make the mistake of giving their plants too much water, especially in winter when the plant is no longer growing and in a dormant state. The signs of overwatering are sodden compost and limpish leaves changing colour to yellow or brown.

How often you decide to water your plants may depend

to some extent on the container. As a general rule, plants in the traditional clay pot need slightly more water than plants growing in plastic pots. To make life really easy, there are now self-watering plant pots on the market. A permeable barrier separates the reservoir from the plant pot but allows the roots to draw up the water. Create your own self-watering container by filling a planter trough with peat. Keep the peat moist and the plants will regulate their own supply of water. The same principle applies to a plastic tray filled with gravel or coloured pebbles.

After the initial cost of buying plant pots and containers for your new indoor plants, the only other essential equipment you'll need is a small watering can with a long spout and a mister to spray pest killers or spread a fine mist to improve humidity around the plants.

MORE HOME HOBBIES

Gardening is a hobby which is directly related to the home. Even indoor plants in pots have to be carefully placed in the correct position in the house to ensure they get the right amount of light and shade, and a well laid-out garden is a pleasure to look at and may also increase the value of your home. There are not many other things you can make yourself which so directly relate to a particular house. However, anything you create will in some way be planned for the particular room in which you wish it to live, so before you begin to make anything, think whether it will be practical and possible to move it later on, or whether you are going to have to leave it behind when you go. You may regret the time and love you poured into something when you discover too late that you can't take it with you.

Having said that, there are many things which are easily transportable, will give you hours of fun, and will provide that special feeling which making your own things always brings. Self-made objects will also add a certain touch of originality and uniqueness to your home, as no one else will have ones quite like them.

The variety of home-based crafts is endless, from restoring old furniture (or building your own from scratch) to making your own beer and preserves. All these activities are highly popular in our mass-market culture, as people like to bring a touch of originality into their lives. There are many good books available on practically every hobby you can imagine, and any good bookstore should have a well-stocked DIY and crafts section. When choosing your hobby, keep in mind the four points mentioned at the beginning of this chapter. Be realistic about the availability of time and space in your home and in your life. Don't try and do more than you can reasonably cope with, or the pleasure will turn into a chore. Don't start with a large project if you've never done it before; you may find that you don't enjoy it. Set yourself small projects in the beginning and work your way up as your interest and skills grow. If you find that you become really keen, there are many associations for hobby enthusiasts where people meet to share their interests and acquire new skills and techniques. If you are already an enthusiast, you may be able to join a local group immediately. This is one of the best ways of getting started in a new neighbourhood. Here are a few suggestions for hobbies you might consider.

Rug making

This is an extremely repetitive and time-consuming hobby requiring little technical skill, but the end result will, hopefully, be a well-made luxurious wool rug costing much less than shop prices. If you are looking for something to do while watching television or listening to the radio, then this hobby is for you. Most kits contain everything you need to complete the rug. The actual pegging tool is called a latch or latchet hook, the yarn is described as thrums, and the patterned base is sometimes called the canvas.

The cost of making a wool rug can be kept to a minimum

by buying the canvas and yarn separately and making your own pattern. Work out a design on a piece of graph paper and then lightly shade in the corresponding squares on the canvas. It is sometimes possible to buy the base and the required quantity of yarn from specialist handicraft stores. If there isn't one in your area, contact manufacturers who produce rug-making kits to see if they will sell yarn and canvas separately through mail order.

Upholstery

The best advice is to tackle something small until the basic techniques of upholstery have been mastered. As confidence grows so, no doubt, will the size of the project. Beginners will certainly benefit from a night-school course in upholstery, or at the very least a pictorial guide which clearly explains the different stages.

Expenses can be reduced by buying materials in bulk and using tools you may already have. An upholsterer's repair kit should include: a tack lifter, which has a claw head to ease out the tacks; a small stripping chisel and mallet; one or two cutting knives with adjustable blades such as Stanley knives; a petite head hammer; a small tack holder which holds the tack in place while it is being driven into the wood (this last item saves fingers from bruising but is not strictly necessary); an assortment of upholstery needles for the different stitching techniques; and a web stretcher, which is used to pull the webbing or base as tight as possible, as otherwise the chair's seat will lose its shape and sag.

Beer and wine making

So many people become home-brew enthusiasts because making your own wine and beer is a relatively cheap and simple procedure with extremely tasty rewards.

Storage space will have to be found for a fermenting bin

when brewing beer and for a demi-john in the case of wine, not to mention somewhere for the bottles. The natural approach to making beer and wine at home involves the use of common garden vegetables, fresh fruits and plants. Beginners may prefer to start off with the mass-produced wine and beer kits because they simplify the actual brewing process, require less equipment and cut down on the waiting time – a very important consideration when it is your first attempt.

The minimum amount of equipment needed with a home-brew beer kit is: sterilising (Campden) tablets; a polythene fermenting bin; a long wooden or plastic spoon to stir the beer; a syphon and, of course, the bottles and tops. For wine kits the equipment list includes: a glass demi-john; a lock and cork, which keeps the airborne vinegar bacteria out but releases the carbon dioxide produced during fermentation; a long tube for syphoning; sterilising (Campden) tablets; and bottles and corks.

Music

Learning to play an instrument can certainly be regarded as a home-based hobby if the would-be musician has had to shelve all musical aspirations because there wasn't room for the baby grand, or the family refused to live with a budding Beethoven.

This might sound a little like putting the cart before the donkey, but if you haven't quite made up your mind as to which instrument to take up (you know it's going to be string, but are still undecided on which one), it might be worth finding out who is actually teaching what in your area. Music teachers often advertise in the local newsagents, library or newspapers. It's much better to know beforehand what's available on your doorstep, rather than spending a small fortune on an instrument and then discovering the nearest tutor lives 25 miles away.

Having decided who to go to for lessons, perhaps the

music teacher might suggest where to look for a suitable instrument, or even come with you to check that you're making a sound investment. After all, he or she will be gaining a pupil.

And to conclude

The challenge of setting up a home lies not only in handling additional responsibilities but also in tackling new hobbies, perhaps even decorating for the first time or attempting a spot of DIY. The keys to your home can also open the door to so many new opportunities. Hopefully, this book has highlighted some of them.